Vishnu's Throne
Shesha, The Serpent King

Table of Contents

Introduction: The Eternal Serpent 2
- Overview of Shesha 2
- Symbolism of Shesha 4
- The Role of Shesha in the Cosmic Cycle 7

Chapter 1: The Origins of Shesha 10
- Shesha in the Vedas 10
- The Birth of Shesha 13
- Shesha's Asceticism 16

Chapter 2: Shesha and the Cosmic Ocean 19
- Ananta, the Infinite One 19
- The Ocean of Milk 21
- Shesha's Role in the Churning of the Ocean 24

Chapter 3: Shesha as Vishnu's Throne 27
- The Divine Throne 27
- The Symbolic Interpretation 30
- Shesha as the Preserver of Dharma 34

Chapter 4: Shesha and the Cycle of Time 38
- The Endless Cycles of Yugas 38
- Shesha and the Kalpa 40
- The Role of Shesha in Pralaya (Cosmic Dissolution) 43

Chapter 5: Shesha and the Avataras of Vishnu 46
- Shesha in the Ramayana 49
- Shesha in the Mahabharata 51

Chapter 6: Shesha in Iconography and Temples 55
- Iconography of Shesha 55
- Temples Dedicated to Shesha 58
- The Serpent King in Modern Devotion 60

Chapter 7: Shesha's Connection with the Naga Kingdom 63
- The Nagas in Hindu Mythology 63

- Patala and the Underworld 67
- Shesha as a Protector of Treasures 70

Chapter 8: Shesha's Place in Hindu Cosmology 73
- The Serpent as a Cosmic Foundation 73
- The Sacred Geometry of Shesha 76
- Shesha and the Multiverse 79

Chapter 9: Shesha and the Mystical Serpents of Other Cultures 83
- Serpent Symbolism Across the World 83
- Shesha and the Kundalini Energy 86
- Shesha in Buddhism and Jainism 90

Chapter 10: The Eternal Legacy of Shesha 92
- Shesha's Role in the Modern World 92
- Lessons from Shesha's Life 95
- Shesha and the Future of Creation 98

Conclusion: The Infinite Protector 101
- The Final Vision of Shesha 101
- The Journey of the Serpent King 103
- Shesha as a Symbol of Cosmic Truth 106

Introduction: The Eternal Serpent

- Overview of Shesha

In the vast and intricate tapestry of Hindu mythology, few figures loom as large and as eternal as Shesha, the Serpent King. Also known as Ananta, which means "the Infinite," Shesha is not merely a deity or a mythological creature; he is the very foundation of the universe itself, embodying the timeless principles of balance, protection, and cosmic order. His presence is felt throughout the sacred scriptures, from the Vedas to the Puranas, and he plays a pivotal role in maintaining the universe, often serving as the divine throne or bed for Lord Vishnu, the preserver of creation. In many ways, Shesha is the silent, eternal witness to the grand cosmic drama, a being whose influence extends far beyond mere myth, touching upon the deepest spiritual truths of existence.

Shesha is not just a serpent; he is **the** serpent, a symbol of continuity, endurance, and eternity. With countless heads, each one holding a world or universe in its gaze, Shesha represents the idea that the cosmos is vast, interconnected, and held together by a force beyond comprehension. His body, coiled infinitely, supports the planets, stars, and galaxies, ensuring that the cosmic order remains intact. Shesha's very existence is a reminder of the unseen forces that hold the universe in balance, forces that are not often noticed but are essential for the stability of all creation.

Shesha's association with Lord Vishnu, one of the three principal deities in the Hindu trinity (Trimurti), elevates his significance in the spiritual and cosmic hierarchy. Vishnu, the preserver of the universe, often reclines upon the coils of Shesha, floating on the primordial ocean of milk (Kshira Sagara) in a state of divine rest between the cycles of creation and destruction. This image of Vishnu resting on Shesha is not merely a depiction of divine leisure but a profound representation of the symbiotic relationship between creation and preservation. Shesha, in this context, is not only Vishnu's bed but also the keeper of the universe, supporting it with his infinite strength and vigilance. As Vishnu preserves the universe, Shesha sustains it, ensuring that the cosmic order, or **dharma**, is maintained.

The role of Shesha in Hindu cosmology is both fundamental and multifaceted. As the **Ananta**, he signifies endless time, eternal space, and the infinite nature of existence. In Hindu thought, time is cyclical rather than linear, and Shesha, by his very nature, encapsulates this endless cycle of birth, death, and rebirth. His coils are often interpreted as the circular nature of time—each loop symbolizing a different yuga (epoch) in the grand cycle of cosmic creation and dissolution. When the universe reaches the end of a **kalpa** (a cosmic day of Brahma), it is Shesha who remains, holding the remnants of the cosmos in his infinite embrace, patiently awaiting the next cycle of creation. This depiction of Shesha as the eternal support of the universe emphasizes the Hindu belief in the cyclical nature of time, where beginnings and endings are simply phases in the ongoing cosmic rhythm.

Shesha's mythology is also deeply intertwined with his role as a **protector**. In many tales, he is described as a serpent who supports the earth on his numerous heads, preventing it from sinking into chaos. His association with protection is not limited to the physical realm but extends into the metaphysical as well. Shesha guards the balance of the universe, ensuring that the forces of creation, preservation, and destruction remain in harmony. His devotion to Lord Vishnu, whom he serves eternally, is a reflection of his unwavering commitment to maintaining this balance. Shesha, in his infinite form, stands as the ultimate protector, safeguarding not just the physical world but the very principles that govern existence.

In Hindu mythology, serpents or **Nagas** hold a complex and revered place, often seen as guardians of treasures, both material and spiritual. Shesha, as the king of the Nagas, represents the pinnacle of this guardian archetype. He is both a physical and spiritual protector, his coils safeguarding the treasures of the cosmos—truth, order, and dharma. The Nagas, including Shesha, are often associated with the **underworld** or **Patala**, a realm beneath the earth. This connection to the underworld further enhances Shesha's role as a protector, not just of the visible universe but of the hidden, unseen forces that govern it. His dominion over Patala represents his authority over the mysterious and the unknown, guarding the foundations of existence from forces that seek to disrupt the cosmic order.

Shesha's **asceticism** is another crucial aspect of his character. According to myth, Shesha renounced worldly desires and performed intense penance to gain the favor of Brahma, the creator god. His penance was so powerful that it caused the earth to tilt under his weight, demonstrating the sheer magnitude of his spiritual power. Moved by his dedication, Brahma granted Shesha the role of supporting the universe, thus elevating him to his position as the cosmic serpent. This aspect of Shesha's story highlights the theme of renunciation and service in Hindu philosophy. Despite his immense power, Shesha is not a figure of aggression or dominance; instead, he is a symbol of humility and service, using his strength to support and protect rather than to control or conquer. His selfless devotion to Vishnu further reinforces this image of Shesha as a being who exists solely to serve the greater good.

The serpent, in many cultures, is a symbol of both life and death, of creation and destruction. In Hinduism, this dual symbolism is embodied in Shesha. While he is primarily associated with preservation and protection, he also plays a role in the destruction of the cosmos at the end of each cycle. As the universe dissolves into chaos, it is Shesha who remains, the eternal witness to the end and the beginning of all things. This duality in Shesha's nature reflects the Hindu understanding of the universe as a place of constant change, where creation and destruction are two sides of the same coin, and where time itself is both an enemy and an ally.

Shesha's role extends beyond mythology into the realm of **spiritual symbolism**. In many Hindu traditions, Shesha is associated with the **Kundalini**, the coiled serpent energy that lies dormant at the base of the spine. When awakened, this energy rises through the chakras, leading to spiritual enlightenment. In this sense, Shesha is not just a figure of mythology but a representation of the potential for spiritual awakening that exists within every individual. His infinite coils are a reminder of the limitless possibilities of the human spirit, and his role as the eternal supporter of Vishnu reflects the idea that divine grace and protection are always available to those who seek it.

In conclusion, Shesha stands as a towering figure in Hindu mythology, not just because of his immense power and eternal nature, but because of the profound spiritual truths he represents. He is the embodiment of eternity, a being who exists beyond time and space, holding the universe together with his infinite strength. His devotion to Vishnu, his role as the cosmic support, and his symbolic connection to the cycles of time and creation make him one of the most important and revered figures in Hindu cosmology. Through his myths, we glimpse the vastness of the universe, the complexity of existence, and the eternal dance of creation and destruction that defines life itself. As the Serpent King, Shesha is more than a protector or a servant; he is the very foundation of the cosmos, an eternal presence that ensures the universe continues to thrive in perfect harmony.

- Symbolism of Shesha

In the grand tapestry of Hindu mythology and philosophy, symbolism plays a pivotal role in conveying deep spiritual truths, moral values, and cosmic principles. Among the myriad figures that populate the sacred stories of ancient India, Shesha, the Serpent King, emerges as one of the most potent and multifaceted symbols. His image, that of a multi-headed serpent coiled infinitely, supporting the universe or serving as the throne for Lord Vishnu, carries a vast and layered symbolism. Each element of Shesha's form, function, and narrative significance reveals profound insights into the nature of existence, time, the universe, and spirituality. To understand Shesha is to delve into the heart of Hindu cosmology, where the serpent king embodies not only the mechanics of the cosmos but also the timeless spiritual journey of the individual soul.

1. Shesha as the Symbol of Infinity and Eternity

The very name **Shesha** means "that which remains," while his alternate name, **Ananta**, means "the Infinite." These names encapsulate one of the most profound aspects of Shesha's symbolism: he represents infinity and the eternal. Shesha is often depicted with his body coiled endlessly, stretching far beyond the limits of mortal comprehension. In this imagery, Shesha symbolizes the idea that the universe is boundless, both in its spatial dimensions and in the cyclical nature of time.

In Hindu cosmology, time is not linear but cyclical, moving through repeated cycles of creation, preservation, and destruction. Shesha, with his endless coils, represents this cyclical concept of time. He exists beyond the temporal constraints of human life, and even beyond the vast time spans of the gods. Shesha's coils can be seen as loops of time, representing the **yugas** (epochs) and **kalpas** (cosmic days and nights) through which the universe continuously flows. Each cycle begins and ends, but Shesha remains, embodying the eternal force that persists through every transformation. This symbolism of eternity is a powerful reminder in Hindu philosophy that although life and the universe are transient, there is something eternal, unchanging, and timeless that underlies all of existence—this eternal essence is symbolized by Shesha.

2. Shesha as the Foundation of the Universe

Another important symbolic role of Shesha is his function as the **foundation of the universe**. In many Hindu texts, Shesha is described as supporting the entire cosmos on his numerous heads, holding the planets and stars in place. This imagery conveys the idea that the universe, despite its vastness and complexity, is supported by a divine, stable foundation. Shesha's infinite form provides the structural stability for the cosmos, much like the physical laws of nature that keep planets in orbit or the unseen forces that hold the fabric of reality together.

The symbolism of Shesha as the cosmic foundation also speaks to the notion of **balance and harmony** in the universe. In Hindu cosmology, the universe is seen as a delicately balanced system, where opposing forces must be in equilibrium for life and creation to flourish. Shesha, with his strong, stable form, represents this cosmic balance. His presence ensures that the planets do not fall into chaos, that the stars do not lose their place in the heavens. He is the unseen force that maintains order amidst the vastness of space. In a metaphysical sense, Shesha symbolizes the principle of **dharma**—the cosmic order, the law that governs not just human conduct but the universe itself. Just as Shesha keeps the universe in balance, dharma ensures that the forces of creation, preservation, and destruction are in harmony.

3. Shesha as the Throne of Vishnu: The Union of Power and Devotion

Perhaps one of the most iconic images of Shesha is his role as the **throne or bed of Lord Vishnu**, where he is often depicted coiled beneath the reclining Vishnu, floating on the cosmic ocean (Kshira Sagara) between the cycles of creation. In this context, Shesha symbolizes both **power** and **service**. On one hand, Shesha is a mighty being in his own right—an infinite serpent with countless heads, representing immense strength and cosmic authority. Yet, on the other hand, Shesha's primary function is to serve Lord Vishnu, the preserver of the universe. This duality makes Shesha a symbol of the perfect union between **power and devotion**.

Shesha's unwavering devotion to Vishnu is a reminder that true power is not about domination or control, but about service to a higher purpose. Shesha, despite his immense strength, exists solely to support Vishnu, who embodies preservation and protection. In this way, Shesha's symbolism teaches the spiritual principle of **selfless service**, or **seva**. His existence is dedicated to maintaining the cosmos, yet he does so without seeking personal gain or recognition. This is a profound lesson in humility and devotion—qualities that are highly valued in Hindu spirituality.

Furthermore, Shesha's position as Vishnu's throne also represents the **spiritual foundation** upon which the divine rests. Vishnu, the preserver, cannot function without the stable, infinite support of Shesha. In this way, Shesha is not just a physical foundation, but a spiritual one as well. He represents the idea that the universe, and even the gods themselves, rest upon deeper spiritual truths that are eternal and unshakable. The **coiled serpent**, with its endless loops, becomes a symbol of the deeper layers of reality that support the material world—a metaphor for the unseen spiritual forces that sustain life.

4. Shesha and the Symbolism of Serpents in Hinduism

In Hindu mythology, serpents or **Nagas** carry rich and complex symbolism. They are often seen as protectors of treasures, both material and spiritual. Shesha, as the king of all Nagas, embodies this protective aspect to its fullest extent. In his role as the supporter of the universe and the servant of Vishnu, Shesha symbolizes the **guardianship** of cosmic treasures—truth, order, and dharma. Serpents, in many ancient cultures, are also associated with **transformation** and **rebirth** due to their ability to shed their skin. Shesha, with his infinite form and his association with the cyclical nature of time, represents the constant transformation of the universe, where life, death, and rebirth are part of the eternal cosmic dance.

Furthermore, serpents in Hinduism often symbolize **kundalini**, the coiled energy that lies dormant at the base of the spine. When awakened, this energy rises through the chakras, leading to spiritual enlightenment. In this sense, Shesha represents not just the physical universe, but the **spiritual potential** that lies within every individual. His infinite form symbolizes the **boundless spiritual energy** that can be awakened within, leading to higher states of consciousness and union with the divine. The symbolism of Shesha as both the cosmic serpent and the kundalini energy highlights the interconnectedness of the material and spiritual worlds, suggesting that the path to spiritual awakening is deeply rooted in the structure of the universe itself.

5. Shesha as a Symbol of Protection and Strength

Shesha's protective role is further emphasized by his ability to shield the universe from chaos. In many depictions, Shesha is shown with his hoods spread wide, covering and protecting Lord Vishnu as he rests between the cycles of creation. This imagery conveys the idea that Shesha is not just a passive foundation for the universe, but an active protector who shields the cosmos from harm. His countless heads and immense strength make him an invincible guardian, capable of defending the universe against any force that might threaten its stability.

This protective symbolism extends beyond the physical realm into the spiritual. Shesha, as the eternal serpent, represents the **spiritual protection** that is available to all beings who seek to live in harmony with the cosmic order. His presence is a reminder that, even in the midst of chaos and destruction, there is a force of protection that sustains life and ensures the continuity of existence. Shesha's protective nature is also symbolic of the **divine grace** that supports and sustains the individual soul, providing strength and stability on the spiritual journey.

6. Shesha and the Symbolism of Patience and Devotion

One of the most remarkable qualities of Shesha is his **unwavering patience**. As the eternal serpent, Shesha remains coiled, supporting the universe through countless cycles of creation and destruction, without complaint or fatigue. This aspect of Shesha's symbolism speaks to the spiritual virtue of patience, particularly in the face of the vast, incomprehensible movements of time and the universe. Shesha's eternal patience reminds us that the cosmic order unfolds according to its own rhythm, and that true wisdom lies in surrendering to this rhythm rather than resisting it.

Shesha's devotion to Vishnu also symbolizes the importance of **bhakti**, or loving devotion to the divine. Despite his immense power and eternal nature, Shesha dedicates himself entirely to the service of Vishnu. This symbolism teaches the spiritual principle that no matter how great one's strength or abilities, the highest path is one of devotion and selfless service. Shesha's eternal devotion to Vishnu serves as a model for all beings, showing that true fulfillment comes not from seeking power or control, but from dedicating oneself to the greater good and the divine will.

Conclusion: The Multilayered Symbolism of Shesha

Shesha, the eternal serpent, stands as one of the most profound symbols in Hindu mythology. He represents the infinite nature of the universe, the cyclical flow of time, and the stability that underpins all creation. As the throne of Vishnu, Shesha embodies the perfect union of power and devotion, teaching that true strength lies in service to the divine. His form, coiled infinitely, symbolizes the endless potential for spiritual awakening and transformation that exists within every being. At the same time, Shesha's protective nature reminds us that there is a force of grace and stability that sustains the universe through even the darkest times. Through Shesha, we are invited to contemplate the vast, eternal forces that shape our existence, and to find strength, patience, and devotion in the face of life's challenges.

In the grand cosmic drama, Shesha remains ever-present, a timeless reminder of the eternal truths that guide both the universe and the human soul. Through his symbolism, we glimpse the deeper layers of reality that exist beyond the material world, and we are reminded of the spiritual journey that lies at the heart of existence—a journey supported and sustained by the infinite, coiled serpent that lies beneath all things.

- The Role of Shesha in the Cosmic Cycle

The cosmic cycle in Hindu cosmology is an eternal dance of creation, preservation, and destruction—an intricate, rhythmic pattern that governs the flow of time and existence. It is within this grand framework that the significance of Shesha, the Serpent King, truly unfolds. More than a mere figure in the pantheon of Hindu mythology, Shesha plays a pivotal role in sustaining and governing the cosmos across its infinite cycles. His presence is both tangible and metaphysical, his influence stretching beyond myth into the very fabric of the universe. The role of Shesha in the cosmic cycle is not only central to Hindu cosmological narratives but also symbolic of the deeper truths of existence, time, and transformation. To understand Shesha is to understand the cosmic rhythms of the universe, the eternal forces that operate within, and the profound spiritual wisdom embedded in the cycles of life.

1. Shesha as the Pillar of Cosmic Stability

At the core of Shesha's role in the cosmic cycle lies his function as the **pillar of stability** upon which the universe rests. In Hindu cosmology, the universe is often described as vast, multi-layered, and cyclical, constantly undergoing phases of creation, sustenance, and dissolution. Amidst this flux, Shesha represents the **unchanging foundation**—a cosmic constant that supports the universe through its many transformations. He is often depicted with his immense coils holding up the planets, stars, and even the very cosmos itself, ensuring that the universe remains stable despite the cyclical nature of time.

This stability is not merely physical, but deeply **metaphysical** as well. Shesha's coils symbolize the hidden laws that govern the universe—the **laws of dharma** (cosmic order), which maintain the balance between creation and destruction. In this sense, Shesha acts as a **regulator of cosmic equilibrium**. His role is to uphold the delicate balance that sustains life, ensuring that the forces of creation and destruction do not overwhelm each other. Without Shesha's stable presence, the universe would fall into chaos, unable to maintain its rhythm of birth, growth, decay, and rebirth.

In essence, Shesha embodies the idea that while the universe is subject to change, there is a deeper, eternal force that underlies and supports it. His presence as the cosmic pillar teaches us that beneath the ever-changing surface of life, there exists a foundation of **eternal truth**, stability, and order—principles that transcend time and space.

2. Shesha and the Cyclical Nature of Time

One of the most important aspects of Shesha's role in the cosmic cycle is his connection to the **cyclical nature of time**. In Hindu cosmology, time is understood as moving in vast, repeating cycles known as **yugas** and **kalpas**. These cycles represent the eternal flow of time, wherein the universe undergoes endless phases of creation (srishti), preservation (sthiti), and destruction (pralaya). Shesha, as the eternal serpent, is intimately connected to this concept of time. His coiled form is often interpreted as a representation of the cyclical nature of the cosmos—an endless loop of creation, dissolution, and rebirth that continues for eternity.

Each cycle of time, or **Maha Yuga**, is composed of four yugas: **Satya Yuga** (the age of truth), **Treta Yuga** (the age of sacrifice), **Dvapara Yuga** (the age of duality), and **Kali Yuga** (the age of strife). These four yugas form a complete cycle, after which the universe undergoes a period of dissolution before being recreated again. Shesha, whose name means "that which remains," is the **eternal witness** to these cosmic cycles. He endures through the ages, his existence transcending the rise and fall of civilizations, gods, and worlds.

In this way, Shesha symbolizes **eternity and continuity** in the midst of constant change. Even as the universe undergoes destruction and rebirth, Shesha remains, embodying the unbroken flow of time. His role in the cosmic cycle is to **anchor time itself**, ensuring that the transitions between the yugas occur smoothly and according to the divine plan. This concept also teaches the philosophical idea that time is cyclical, not linear, and that all things—whether material, spiritual, or cosmic—are part of a larger, repeating cycle of existence.

3. Shesha and the Cosmic Ocean: The Transition Between Cycles

One of the most iconic depictions of Shesha is his presence in the **cosmic ocean**, where he serves as the throne or bed for Lord Vishnu, the preserver of the universe. In this image, Vishnu rests on Shesha during the intervals between the cycles of creation, floating on the **Kshira Sagara** (the Ocean of Milk), a primordial ocean that symbolizes the unmanifest potential of the universe. This depiction of Shesha as the resting place for Vishnu holds profound symbolic meaning within the context of the cosmic cycle.

The cosmic ocean represents the **state of dissolution** (pralaya), a period of rest when the universe is withdrawn into its latent form, awaiting the next cycle of creation. During this phase, all of creation is reabsorbed into the primordial waters, and time itself enters a state of suspended animation. Shesha, however, remains—floating on the ocean, supporting Vishnu, and waiting for the moment when the next cycle will begin. This imagery emphasizes Shesha's role as the **custodian of cosmic potential**, holding the universe in a state of balance during the transition between cycles.

In this context, Shesha symbolizes **continuity** amidst the temporary dissolution of the universe. Even as the cosmos dissolves back into its primordial state, Shesha's presence signifies that the forces of creation are merely in a state of dormancy, ready to reemerge at the appointed time. His role as Vishnu's throne during these periods of cosmic rest underscores the idea that the preservation and maintenance of the universe require both **stability and patience**. It also reflects the **eternal nature of the soul**, which, like the universe, undergoes cycles of birth, death, and rebirth, but remains fundamentally eternal and unchanging.

4. Shesha and the Role of Destruction in the Cosmic Cycle

Although Shesha is primarily associated with the stability and preservation of the cosmos, his role in the cosmic cycle also includes a symbolic connection to **destruction and renewal**. In Hindu cosmology, destruction is not seen as negative, but as an essential part of the cosmic process, allowing for the renewal and regeneration of the universe. Shesha's association with **destruction** comes from his connection to **Lord Shiva**, the god of destruction and transformation, who also has ties to serpents and the cyclical nature of the cosmos.

In some texts, Shesha is described as a servant of Shiva during the process of **pralaya**, when the universe is dissolved into chaos. During this time, Shesha helps to **reabsorb** the cosmic energies, preparing the universe for its eventual recreation. His role in this process reflects the idea that destruction is not an end, but a necessary step in the cycle of creation. By participating in this process, Shesha embodies the principle of **cosmic transformation**, where old forms must be broken down to make way for new ones.

This aspect of Shesha's symbolism also speaks to the **transformative power of destruction** on a personal and spiritual level. Just as the universe must undergo periods of dissolution, so too must individuals experience phases of personal transformation, where old patterns, habits, and attachments are shed to allow for spiritual growth. Shesha's presence in the cycle of destruction serves as a reminder that even in times of chaos and dissolution, there is an underlying force of stability and continuity that ensures the eventual rebirth of the soul and the cosmos.

5. Shesha as the Guardian of Cosmic Knowledge

Another important role of Shesha in the cosmic cycle is his function as the **guardian of cosmic knowledge**. In Hindu mythology, serpents are often seen as symbols of **wisdom and hidden knowledge**, and Shesha, as the king of serpents, is no exception. He is believed to possess the knowledge of the universe's creation, its cycles, and the deeper laws that govern existence. In this role, Shesha acts as a **repository of cosmic secrets**, a being who holds the wisdom of the ages and ensures that this knowledge is preserved across the cycles of time.

Shesha's connection to **cosmic wisdom** is particularly evident in his relationship with Lord Vishnu. As Vishnu's eternal companion and throne, Shesha is privy to the divine plans for the universe, understanding the intricate workings of creation, preservation, and destruction. This places Shesha in the unique position of being both a participant in the cosmic cycle and a **witness to its deeper mysteries**.

In some versions of the mythology, Shesha is said to recite the **Vedas**—the ancient scriptures of Hinduism—while supporting the universe. This act of recitation symbolizes the transmission of divine knowledge across the ages, ensuring that the eternal truths of existence are never lost, even as the universe undergoes its many transformations. In this way, Shesha serves as a symbol of **spiritual wisdom**, teaching us that the key to understanding the cosmic cycle lies in the knowledge of the eternal principles that govern life, death, and rebirth.

6. Shesha and the Cycles of Individual Existence

While Shesha's role in the cosmic cycle is vast and universal, his symbolism also extends to the **individual level**, particularly in the context of the soul's journey through life and death. Just as the universe undergoes cycles of creation and dissolution, so too does the individual soul (atman) experience **cycles of birth, death, and rebirth** (samsara). Shesha's role as the eternal serpent mirrors this process, symbolizing the continuous journey of the soul through the cycles of existence.

In Hindu thought, the goal of spiritual practice is to transcend the cycles of samsara and attain **moksha**—liberation from the cycle of birth and death. Shesha's presence as a figure who transcends time and the cosmic cycles offers a powerful symbol for the spiritual aspirant. His ability to remain eternal, even as the universe is dissolved and recreated, represents the soul's potential for **liberation** and **eternal existence** beyond the cycles of samsara.

Shesha's connection to **yoga** also speaks to his role in the individual's spiritual journey. In many depictions, Shesha is shown coiled in a manner that resembles the yogic postures associated with **kundalini energy**—the dormant spiritual energy believed to reside at the base of the spine. Just as Shesha holds the universe within his coils, the awakened kundalini energy rises through the chakras, leading the practitioner toward spiritual enlightenment. In this sense, Shesha's role in the cosmic cycle parallels the spiritual journey of awakening and liberation, offering a profound metaphor for the path toward moksha.

Conclusion

Shesha's role in the cosmic cycle is as profound as it is multifaceted. As the eternal serpent, he represents stability, continuity, and wisdom amidst the ever-changing rhythms of the universe. His presence as the support of Lord Vishnu during the cosmic intervals emphasizes the eternal nature of the divine plan, while his connection to the cycles of time and destruction underscores the transformative power of change. Through Shesha, we are reminded that the universe operates according to an eternal rhythm—one that governs both the cosmos and the individual soul. In understanding his role, we glimpse the deeper truths of existence, and the timeless forces that guide us through the cycles of life, death, and rebirth.

Chapter 1: The Origins of Shesha

- Shesha in the Vedas

The roots of Shesha, the primordial serpent in Hindu mythology, stretch deep into the ancient Vedic texts, the foundation of Hindu religious thought. To explore Shesha's origins within the Vedas is to journey back to the earliest spiritual literature of India, where the cosmic serpents—known as **nāgas**—appear as symbols of the primal forces of nature, guardians of secret wisdom, and embodiments of cosmic power. Although Shesha as we understand him today—coiled beneath Lord Vishnu, holding up the universe—takes more defined shape in later texts such as the **Mahabharata** and the **Puranas**, the Vedic scriptures provide the initial framework from which this great serpent emerges.

The Vedas, particularly the **Rigveda**, introduce us to a worldview in which serpentine deities and forces occupy a central role in the structure of the cosmos. Shesha's essence, like many key figures of Hindu mythology, begins here, in the hymns that explore the mysteries of creation, cosmic order, and the balance of the universe. Although the specific name "Shesha" may not be explicitly mentioned in the earliest Vedic texts, the foundations for understanding his significance—his nature as a serpent, his cosmic role, and his symbolism—are laid out with vivid imagery and metaphysical concepts. To fully grasp Shesha's origins, one must delve into the rich layers of Vedic thought, where serpentine forces are interwoven with the primal energies that sustain the cosmos.

1. The Vedic Serpents: The Archetype of Cosmic Power

The Vedas are filled with references to **serpentine forces**, most commonly represented by the nāgas— powerful serpent beings who dwell in the waters, the earth, and the heavens. The Vedic nāgas are beings of immense power, often associated with both the nurturing and destructive aspects of nature. They control the flow of rivers, preside over the fertility of the earth, and, at times, are linked to storms and cosmic upheavals. Although Shesha, in his later form, is typically seen as a protector and sustainer, his Vedic roots tie him to these primordial nāgas, whose power is both creative and potentially destructive.

One of the earliest Vedic references to serpentine forces can be found in the **Rigveda**, in hymns dedicated to the god **Indra** and his battle with the serpent **Vritra**. Vritra is a cosmic serpent, often described as a demon or asura, who holds back the waters of creation, causing drought and chaos. Indra, the king of the gods, is celebrated for his victory over Vritra, releasing the waters and restoring cosmic order. While Vritra is ultimately defeated, his form as a serpent points to the dual nature of serpentine beings in the Vedic worldview: they are both the guardians of life-giving waters and the harbingers of chaos.

In this context, Shesha can be seen as evolving from this archetype of the cosmic serpent—a being who embodies both the **primal energy of creation** and the **potential for destruction**. Unlike Vritra, Shesha is not an antagonist; rather, he represents the controlled and benevolent aspect of serpentine power. His role as the support of the universe and the bed of Lord Vishnu suggests that, in Shesha, the cosmic serpent's power has been harnessed for the purpose of sustaining and protecting creation. This shift from the chaotic serpentine forces of the Vedic age to the stabilizing figure of Shesha marks an important evolution in Hindu cosmology.

2. Shesha and the Vedic Symbolism of Serpents

In Vedic thought, serpents are often symbolic of the **cyclical nature of existence**—particularly the cycles of life, death, and rebirth. The image of a serpent shedding its skin is a powerful metaphor for renewal and transformation, and this imagery is woven into the fabric of Vedic cosmology. The cyclical nature of the serpent is closely tied to the Vedic conception of time, which is seen not as linear, but as an endless series of cycles. Shesha's role in later Hindu mythology—as the eternal serpent who survives through the dissolution and recreation of the universe—has its conceptual roots in this Vedic understanding of time and renewal.

In the **Atharvaveda**, there are hymns that speak of the **serpent's connection to immortality**, a concept that foreshadows Shesha's eternal nature. The serpent is seen as a being that transcends the ordinary boundaries of life and death, existing in a state of perpetual renewal. This association with immortality also links serpents to the idea of **divine knowledge** and **hidden wisdom**. The serpent, dwelling in the depths of the earth and the waters, is a symbol of the mysteries of creation, the secrets of life, and the hidden truths of the universe. In later traditions, Shesha is often depicted as the repository of cosmic knowledge, a being who understands the deeper truths of existence. This theme is echoed in the Vedas, where serpents are often invoked in rituals seeking protection, wisdom, and longevity.

One particularly significant Vedic serpent is the **Sarpa**, a term used to refer to snakes or serpentine beings in general. In the **Yajurveda**, Sarpa is described as both feared and revered, embodying the dual nature of serpentine power. The Sarpa is invoked in hymns for protection against its venomous bite, but it is also respected as a guardian of treasures—both material and spiritual. This dual nature of the serpent as both protector and potential destroyer is key to understanding Shesha's later role in Hindu cosmology. Shesha, as the king of serpents, represents the ultimate reconciliation of these two aspects, embodying the controlled, protective aspect of serpentine energy that sustains the cosmos.

3. The Cosmic Serpent and the Waters of Creation

One of the most important themes in the Vedic conception of serpentine forces is their association with the **primordial waters**—the vast, unformed ocean from which all of creation emerges. In the Vedic texts, water is seen as the source of life, the primordial element from which the universe is born. Serpents, as inhabitants of these waters, are intimately connected to the creative forces of the cosmos. They are often depicted as the **guardians of the waters**, holding back the floods until the appropriate time for creation.

This association between serpents and the waters of creation finds its most direct expression in the figure of **Vritra**, who, as mentioned earlier, withholds the life-giving waters, only to be defeated by Indra. However, in other hymns, serpents are seen as more benevolent forces, guarding the sacred rivers and ensuring the flow of life-giving waters. This duality is key to understanding the later role of Shesha, who exists in the cosmic ocean as the supporter of Lord Vishnu during the intervals between the cycles of creation. Shesha's presence in the cosmic waters symbolizes the controlled release of creative energy—his coils hold the potential for creation in balance, ensuring that the universe is preserved and maintained.

In this sense, Shesha's Vedic roots are tied to the concept of **cosmic balance**. The primordial waters represent both chaos and potential, and the serpent's role is to regulate this energy, allowing creation to unfold according to divine will. Shesha, as the cosmic serpent, continues this role in later texts, where he serves as both a **protector of the universe** and a **regulator of cosmic forces**. His presence in the cosmic ocean during the periods of dissolution (pralaya) suggests that, even in the midst of chaos, there is a force that maintains balance and ensures the eventual recreation of the universe.

4. Shesha's Emergence from the Vedic Nāga Tradition

While Shesha's fully formed character emerges in the later Puranic and epic texts, his origins can be traced to the broader Vedic tradition of **nāgas**, serpent deities who play important roles in both the material and spiritual realms. The nāgas of the Vedic period are often depicted as both **guardians of treasures** and **protectors of the waters**, suggesting a dual role as keepers of both material wealth and spiritual knowledge. Shesha, as the king of nāgas, inherits this dual role, becoming not only the protector of the cosmos but also the guardian of cosmic knowledge and spiritual truth.

In the **Rigveda**, there are several references to the **cosmic serpent** as a being who upholds the heavens and the earth. Although these references do not specifically mention Shesha by name, they provide a conceptual framework for understanding his later role as the serpent who supports the universe. The idea of a cosmic serpent who holds the world in balance is deeply rooted in Vedic cosmology, and this theme is later expanded upon in the Puranas, where Shesha's coils are said to uphold the planets and the stars.

In this way, Shesha's origins in the Vedas are linked to the broader **nāga tradition**, which sees serpents as powerful, benevolent forces that play a crucial role in maintaining the order of the cosmos. Shesha, as the supreme nāga, represents the culmination of this tradition, embodying the qualities of protection, stability, and cosmic wisdom that are central to the Vedic conception of serpentine power.

5. The Vedic Seeds of Shesha's Eternal Nature

One of the defining characteristics of Shesha in later mythology is his **eternal nature**—he is the serpent who survives through the dissolution and recreation of the universe, witnessing the cycles of time unfold. This theme of eternity is also present in the Vedic texts, where serpents are often associated with the idea of **immortality** and **timelessness**. In the **Atharvaveda**, there are references to serpents who are invoked for protection against death and disease, suggesting that serpents were seen as beings who could transcend the ordinary limitations of life.

This connection between serpents and immortality foreshadows Shesha's later role as the eternal serpent who exists beyond the boundaries of time. In the Vedic worldview, time is cyclical, and the serpent—who sheds its skin and is reborn—serves as a powerful symbol of this endless cycle of renewal. Shesha's presence at the beginning and end of each cosmic cycle reinforces this theme of eternity, as he is the being who endures through the dissolution and recreation of the universe.

In this way, the Vedic texts provide the seeds for understanding Shesha's role in later Hindu cosmology. The serpentine forces described in the Vedas embody the primal energies of the cosmos—energies that are both creative and destructive, benevolent and fearsome. Shesha, as the eternal serpent, represents the culmination of these forces, embodying the cosmic balance that sustains the universe through the cycles of time.

Conclusion

Shesha's origins in the Vedic texts are deeply intertwined with the ancient Hindu understanding of serpentine forces as cosmic powers that regulate the cycles of creation, destruction, and renewal. While the specific figure of Shesha may not be explicitly named in the Vedas, the conceptual framework for his later role is clearly present in the hymns that celebrate the power of serpents, the mysteries of the primordial waters, and the eternal cycles of time. From these early beginnings, Shesha emerges as the supreme cosmic serpent—the being who supports the universe and holds the key to its balance, continuity, and renewal. Through his Vedic roots, Shesha represents the eternal truth of the cosmos: that even in the midst of change, there is a force that maintains order and sustains life, guiding the universe through its endless cycles.

- The Birth of Shesha

The birth of Shesha, the mighty and eternal serpent, is a deeply significant event in Hindu mythology, intertwined with the themes of cosmic balance, divine purpose, and the origins of the universe itself. Shesha's birth is not merely the emergence of a powerful serpent being, but the manifestation of one of the most vital forces in creation—one that embodies stability, endurance, and the very foundation upon which the cosmos rests. To fully understand the profound nature of Shesha's birth, it is necessary to explore the mythological narratives, the symbolic meanings associated with his creation, and the intricate web of relationships that link him to the greater cosmic order.

Shesha, often referred to as **Ananta-Shesha**, meaning "endless Shesha," is depicted as a serpent of immense size and power, with countless heads adorned with hoods. His birth marks the beginning of his eternal role as the cosmic serpent who supports Lord Vishnu, the preserver of the universe, and holds the cosmos together with his unbreakable strength. Shesha's emergence from the divine waters of creation represents not only the birth of a being of great power, but also the birth of an eternal principle that sustains the universe across the cycles of creation, destruction, and renewal.

1. Shesha's Divine Lineage

To understand the birth of Shesha, one must first explore his divine lineage, which situates him within a broader context of cosmic serpents and divine beings. According to Hindu mythology, Shesha is the eldest of the **naga** brothers, born from the union of **Sage Kashyapa** and his wife **Kadru**, the mother of serpents. Kashyapa, one of the ancient progenitors (Prajapatis), is a sage of immense wisdom and power, while Kadru is one of the daughters of Daksha, a prominent figure in Hindu cosmology known for fathering many divine beings.

Kadru and Kashyapa gave birth to numerous serpents (nagas), with Shesha being the most prominent and eldest among them. His siblings include notable nagas such as **Vasuki**, who would later become famous for his role in the **churning of the ocean** (Samudra Manthan), and **Takshaka**, a serpent king known for his role in the Mahabharata. From the moment of his birth, Shesha was destined to play a role far greater than any of his siblings, not merely as a king of the nagas, but as a being whose very existence was tied to the structure of the cosmos.

The nagas, serpentine beings, are often associated with both the earth and the waters, embodying the primal forces of nature. They are regarded as both protectors and, at times, tempters, capable of great power but also possessing a dual nature—protective and destructive. In this context, Shesha's birth from Kadru places him within this lineage of powerful cosmic serpents, yet he stands apart as the most disciplined, virtuous, and spiritually elevated of his kind. His birth marks the beginning of a journey that would lead him to transcend the dual nature of serpents and assume the role of the ultimate **sustainer** and **guardian** of the universe.

2. Shesha's Spiritual Austerity and the Rejection of Worldly Power

The birth of Shesha, while remarkable in itself, is followed by a crucial period in which he distances himself from his siblings and worldly desires. Shesha's siblings, many of whom are depicted as being consumed by greed and the desire for power, often engaged in conflicts and misdeeds that led to their downfall. Unlike his brothers, Shesha's temperament from birth was marked by an inclination toward **spiritual austerity** and **self-discipline**. This fundamental difference in nature set the stage for his ultimate role as a divine being of immense responsibility.

Disillusioned with the constant bickering and materialism of his naga brethren, Shesha chose a path of renunciation. He withdrew from the world and embarked on a long and arduous journey of **tapasya** (austerity and meditation), seeking to rid himself of all ego, desire, and attachment. It is said that Shesha performed such intense penance that the fire of his spiritual practice threatened to disturb the very balance of the cosmos. His penance was so great that even the gods took notice, realizing that Shesha's devotion and self-control were of a magnitude rarely seen in the universe.

Shesha's rejection of worldly power is a crucial aspect of his character and his cosmic role. While his brothers sought to establish dominion over earthly and material realms, Shesha's renunciation of these desires enabled him to transcend the limits of ordinary beings, even those as powerful as the nagas. His birth, followed by this intense period of spiritual growth, symbolizes the triumph of spiritual discipline over material ambition, a theme that echoes throughout Hindu philosophy.

3. Shesha's Role in Maintaining Cosmic Balance

The culmination of Shesha's spiritual austerities leads to a pivotal moment when he is approached by the gods, who recognize his immense potential. It is said that **Brahma**, the creator of the universe, appeared before Shesha and, in admiration of his unwavering discipline and penance, offered him a boon. Brahma understood that Shesha's power, born of his deep spirituality and detachment from worldly desires, was a force that could be used to support and sustain the very fabric of the universe.

Shesha's request to Brahma was simple yet profound: he wished to dedicate himself to the service of **Lord Vishnu**, the preserver of the cosmos. Shesha understood that Vishnu's role in maintaining cosmic order was of paramount importance, and he desired nothing more than to serve as the foundation upon which Vishnu could rest. In this act of selfless devotion, Shesha cemented his place as the ultimate **sustainer**, offering his body as the bed for Vishnu to rest upon during the periods between the cycles of creation.

From this moment, Shesha was given the responsibility of holding up the entire universe. His countless heads support the planets, the stars, and all of creation, ensuring that the cosmos remains in balance. Shesha's **infinite coils** are said to contain the entire universe, symbolizing the eternal and unchanging nature of the divine order. The image of Vishnu reclining upon Shesha, floating upon the cosmic ocean, represents the harmony between preservation and support—Vishnu preserves the universe, while Shesha provides the foundation upon which that preservation can take place.

4. Shesha's Immortality and the Cycles of Creation

One of the defining characteristics of Shesha is his **immortality**. As the eternal serpent, Shesha survives through the cycles of cosmic creation and dissolution (known as **Kalpas**). When the universe is destroyed at the end of a cosmic cycle, Shesha remains, coiled in the vast cosmic ocean, awaiting the next act of creation. His immortality is a symbol of the eternal nature of the universe itself, which is constantly being created, sustained, and destroyed in an endless cycle.

Shesha's immortality also represents the concept of **eternal support**. Even when the universe dissolves into chaos, Shesha continues to exist, holding the potential for creation within his coils. This idea reflects the Hindu belief in the cyclical nature of time and existence, where the end of one cycle is merely the beginning of another. Shesha's presence ensures that, no matter how many times the universe is destroyed, there is always a foundation upon which it can be rebuilt.

In this way, Shesha is not just a participant in the cosmic cycle—he is one of its key pillars. His birth, followed by his role as the supporter of the universe, symbolizes the **permanence of divine order** in the midst of cosmic impermanence. While the material world may come and go, Shesha, like Vishnu, endures, ensuring that the fundamental structure of the universe remains intact.

5. The Symbolism of Shesha's Birth

The birth of Shesha is steeped in rich symbolism, much of which revolves around the themes of **stability, endurance, and spiritual discipline**. Shesha, with his infinite coils and countless heads, is the embodiment of support and strength, qualities that are crucial to the preservation of the universe. His association with Lord Vishnu further emphasizes his role as a stabilizing force, as Vishnu's own role as the preserver of the cosmos depends on the foundation that Shesha provides.

Shesha's birth from Kadru, the mother of serpents, links him to the primal forces of nature, particularly the earth and water. Serpents in Hindu mythology are often associated with the earth, as they dwell in its depths and are seen as guardians of its treasures. However, Shesha's role as the cosmic serpent elevates him beyond the confines of the material world, positioning him as a protector of the entire universe, not just the earth.

The countless heads of Shesha, each crowned with a protective hood, represent the **multifaceted nature of reality**. In his form, Shesha holds up not just the physical universe, but the different dimensions of existence, including the material, spiritual, and cosmic realms. His ability to support the entire universe on his heads symbolizes the **balance of opposing forces**—light and darkness, creation and destruction, movement and stillness—that make up the cosmos.

Shesha's **infinite form** is a direct reflection of his name, "Ananta," which means "endless" or "infinite." His birth, therefore, is not just the emergence of a powerful being, but the birth of the eternal principle of **support and preservation** that sustains the universe throughout all time. His infinite coils represent the unbroken continuity of the universe, while his countless heads signify the many facets of existence that are held together by his strength.

Conclusion

The birth of Shesha is one of the most significant events in Hindu mythology, not just because it marks the beginning of his role as the cosmic serpent, but because it symbolizes the emergence of one of the most fundamental principles of the universe: the principle of **support** and **stability**. Through his rejection of worldly desires, his intense spiritual discipline, and his ultimate devotion to Lord Vishnu, Shesha rises above the material world to become the foundation upon which the entire cosmos rests.

In Shesha's birth and subsequent role, we see the embodiment of the eternal truths that govern the universe. Just as the cosmos must be sustained by a force that transcends time and space, so too does Shesha represent the **eternal support** that underpins all of creation. His infinite coils and countless heads hold up not only the physical world, but the very essence of existence itself, ensuring that the universe remains in balance and that the cycles of creation and destruction can continue without interruption. Through Shesha, we are reminded of the **enduring nature of divine order** and the **stability** that supports all of life.

- Shesha's Asceticism

Shesha, the divine serpent king and the eternal bed of Lord Vishnu, is not merely a figure of cosmic grandeur; he is also a profound symbol of asceticism, self-control, and detachment. While Shesha is often depicted in his majestic form with countless hoods, supporting the universe and providing a resting place for Vishnu, the journey to this exalted role was one of rigorous spiritual discipline. Shesha's asceticism, his renunciation of worldly desires, and his pursuit of higher truths form the bedrock of his divine purpose. It is through his unparalleled austerities and penances that Shesha transcends the limitations of his naga lineage and becomes a symbol of cosmic balance and eternal support.

Asceticism, in Hinduism, is the conscious rejection of material attachments in favor of spiritual growth. It is the practice of self-discipline and denial that allows one to transcend the ego, desires, and the bondage of the physical world. Shesha's life exemplifies the highest form of asceticism, where the complete renunciation of worldly power and desires becomes the pathway to cosmic responsibility. His asceticism is not a mere personal pursuit of spiritual enlightenment, but an act of universal significance—one that enables him to sustain the cosmos itself.

1. The Early Struggles: Shesha's Discontent with Worldly Affairs

Born into the powerful race of **nagas**, Shesha was surrounded by siblings who were consumed by greed, ambition, and the desire for domination. The **nagas**, serpentine beings known for their strength and mystique, were often associated with both the earth and the waters, embodying the primal forces of nature. However, while many of his siblings, such as **Vasuki** and **Takshaka**, pursued earthly power, Shesha from the very beginning exhibited a nature that was markedly different. Even as a young naga, Shesha felt a deep discontent with the endless squabbles, rivalries, and materialism that surrounded him.

His brothers and other nagas frequently engaged in acts that were driven by ego, such as seeking wealth, power, and control over the earth and its treasures. This materialistic pursuit often led them to conflicts with both humans and gods. Shesha, however, was repulsed by the greed and destructiveness that he saw in his siblings. From an early age, he recognized that the pursuit of power and dominance brought only suffering, both to those who sought it and to the world around them.

This discontent with worldly affairs became the seed of Shesha's asceticism. He realized that true power did not come from material wealth or control over others, but from self-mastery and the transcendence of desire. Shesha's withdrawal from the affairs of the nagas marked the beginning of his spiritual journey. His renunciation of the world was not a rejection of his duty, but a realization that his true purpose lay far beyond the temporal concerns of his naga brethren.

2. The Great Renunciation: Shesha's Decision to Pursue Tapasya

Shesha's decision to renounce the material world and embark on a path of **tapasya** (austerity and meditation) was both profound and transformative. Tapasya, in Hindu thought, is the rigorous discipline of mind and body through intense meditation, fasting, and self-denial. It is believed to generate immense spiritual power (tapas), which can lead to enlightenment, liberation, or the fulfillment of divine purposes.

Shesha's tapasya was not driven by a desire for personal gain or even for the traditional goal of liberation from the cycle of birth and death. Instead, Shesha's austerities were performed with a singular purpose: to attain a state of complete detachment from all worldly desires and to offer himself in service to **Lord Vishnu**, the preserver of the cosmos. Shesha realized that his true calling was to serve as the eternal support for Vishnu and to assist in maintaining the balance of the universe.

Shesha's renunciation was absolute. He gave up not only material wealth and power but also the pleasures of the senses, the desires of the mind, and the attachments of the heart. His tapasya involved deep meditation that took him beyond the dualities of pleasure and pain, gain and loss, and success and failure.

He meditated for eons, often withdrawing into the deepest recesses of the earth or the cosmic ocean, where he was undisturbed by the distractions of the world.

The fire of Shesha's tapasya was so intense that it began to affect the balance of the universe itself. His penance generated such immense spiritual heat that it threatened to consume the very fabric of existence. Recognizing the magnitude of Shesha's asceticism, the gods, led by **Brahma**, the creator, took notice. They understood that Shesha's tapasya was not merely a personal pursuit of enlightenment but an act that could reshape the cosmic order.

3. The Boon of Brahma: Asceticism as the Key to Cosmic Responsibility

Impressed by Shesha's unwavering dedication and his mastery over the senses, Brahma appeared before him and offered him a boon. Brahma recognized that Shesha's spiritual power was unparalleled and that his self-discipline had made him worthy of any request. In this moment, Shesha demonstrated the true depth of his asceticism. Unlike many ascetics who seek liberation or worldly boons, Shesha asked for nothing for himself. Instead, he requested only one thing: the opportunity to serve **Lord Vishnu**.

Shesha's request to serve as the bed upon which Vishnu could rest during the cosmic cycles of creation and dissolution was a reflection of his selfless devotion and his realization of his higher purpose. He did not desire liberation, wealth, or even divine powers. He sought only to dedicate himself to the preservation of the universe, knowing that Vishnu's role as the preserver depended on a stable foundation.

Brahma, moved by Shesha's humility and his selfless desire, granted his request. He bestowed upon Shesha the boon of immortality, ensuring that Shesha would remain eternal, unchanging, and ever-present, regardless of the cycles of creation and destruction. In granting this boon, Brahma acknowledged that Shesha's asceticism had elevated him to a status beyond even the gods. Shesha had become not only a divine being but a cosmic principle—the very embodiment of support, endurance, and stability.

4. Shesha's Role as the Cosmic Ascetic

Shesha's asceticism did not end with the granting of Brahma's boon. Even in his role as the cosmic serpent who supports the universe, Shesha continues to embody the principles of asceticism. His life is one of eternal service, and his very existence is a testament to the power of renunciation and self-control.

As the **bed of Vishnu**, Shesha exists in a state of perpetual meditation, his mind free from distractions, his body coiled in infinite loops that hold up the cosmos. Shesha's countless heads, each crowned with a protective hood, are symbolic of his omniscient awareness, which allows him to maintain the balance of the universe while remaining detached from its vicissitudes. His coils are said to contain the entire universe, and his unbreakable strength ensures that the cosmos remains in harmony.

Shesha's life as the cosmic ascetic is marked by his complete detachment from all desires. He has no need for food, sleep, or sensory pleasures. His existence is one of pure spiritual discipline, where his only focus is on supporting Vishnu and maintaining the balance of creation. Shesha's asceticism is not just a personal practice; it is a cosmic necessity. Without his tapasya, the universe would lose its foundation, and chaos would ensue.

5. The Symbolism of Shesha's Asceticism

Shesha's asceticism is rich with symbolic meaning, much of which relates to the themes of **stability, endurance, and self-mastery**. His renunciation of worldly desires and his focus on spiritual discipline are symbolic of the highest form of asceticism, where the ego is transcended, and the self is dedicated entirely to the service of a higher purpose.

Shesha's coils, which support the universe, represent the **infinite power** that can be generated through asceticism. Just as Shesha's coils are unbreakable and eternal, so too is the power of tapasya when practiced with pure intention and selflessness. His countless heads, each watching over a different aspect of the cosmos, symbolize the **omniscience** that comes with spiritual mastery. Shesha's ability to maintain the balance of the universe while remaining detached from it represents the ideal of **detachment in action**—a key concept in Hindu philosophy.

Moreover, Shesha's asceticism highlights the **cyclical nature of time** and the **eternal continuity of the universe**. His ability to exist beyond the cycles of creation and destruction reflects the idea that true spiritual power transcends the temporal world. Shesha, as the cosmic ascetic, exists outside the boundaries of time, embodying the eternal principles that govern the cosmos.

6. Shesha's Asceticism and the Path to Moksha

Shesha's asceticism also serves as a model for those on the path to **moksha** (liberation). While Shesha himself did not seek personal liberation, his tapasya demonstrates the transformative power of self-discipline and renunciation. By giving up worldly desires and dedicating oneself to a higher purpose, one can attain spiritual liberation, just as Shesha transcended his naga nature and became a cosmic force.

Shesha's life reminds us that asceticism is not about denying the world for the sake of denial itself, but about freeing oneself from the bonds of desire in order to realize one's true purpose. For Shesha, this purpose was to support Vishnu and maintain the balance of the universe. For others, it may be the pursuit of spiritual enlightenment or the fulfillment of their dharma. In either case, the path of asceticism is one of **self-mastery, detachment, and devotion**.

Conclusion

Shesha's asceticism is a testament to the transformative power of self-discipline, renunciation, and spiritual dedication. His journey from a naga disillusioned with worldly affairs to the cosmic serpent who supports the entire universe is a profound illustration of the potential that lies within each being to transcend their limitations and realize their highest purpose. Through his tapasya, Shesha not only attained immortality but became a symbol of cosmic stability and divine support. His asceticism continues to inspire, reminding us of the eternal truths that govern the universe and the power of selflessness in the pursuit of higher goals.

Chapter 2: Shesha and the Cosmic Ocean

• Ananta, the Infinite One

In the vast expanse of Hindu mythology, few beings embody the essence of infinity as profoundly as Shesha, also known as Ananta, the Infinite One. Ananta, whose name literally translates to "endless" or "infinite," is not merely a figure of myth but a symbol of the boundless and eternal nature of the cosmos. He is often depicted as an immense serpent, coiled endlessly in the cosmic ocean, supporting the universe upon his many hoods. Shesha, in his manifestation as Ananta, represents the unbroken continuity of existence, the eternal support that upholds creation, preservation, and even the dissolution of the universe.

The Cosmic Ocean and the Infinite Coils

Ananta's association with the cosmic ocean is a powerful symbol of his role in the cosmos. In Hindu cosmology, the cosmic ocean is not just a vast body of water but a representation of the primordial state of existence—an endless, uncharted expanse that predates the creation of the universe. It is in this infinite, unfathomable ocean that Shesha lies, his countless coils forming an unshakable foundation for all of creation. Each coil represents a different aspect of time and space, interwoven in such a way that they seamlessly sustain the cosmic order. As the serpent of infinity, Ananta does not merely exist within this ocean; he is an intrinsic part of it, embodying the timeless, boundless nature of the universe itself.

Shesha's Role as the Bed of Vishnu

In the rich tapestry of Hindu mythological narratives, Shesha, as Ananta, is often depicted as the bed upon which Lord Vishnu, the preserver of the universe, reclines. This imagery is deeply symbolic, reflecting the concept that Vishnu, as the preserver, rests upon the eternal and unchanging foundation of existence represented by Shesha. The serene posture of Vishnu on the serpent's coils suggests a state of cosmic equilibrium, a harmonious balance maintained by the infinite nature of Ananta. It is said that during the intervals between cosmic cycles, Vishnu lies in deep meditation on Ananta, floating on the Kshira Sagara, the ocean of milk, symbolizing the suspension of the universe between periods of creation and dissolution. In this tranquil state, Shesha supports not just Vishnu, but the very essence of continuity and stability in the cosmos.

Ananta and the Cycles of Time

Shesha's infinite nature also connects deeply with the Hindu understanding of time, known as Kala. Time in Hindu philosophy is not linear but cyclical, encompassing endless cycles of creation (Srishti), preservation (Sthiti), and destruction (Pralaya). Ananta, as the embodiment of infinity, transcends these cycles, existing beyond the limitations of time. His presence in the cosmic ocean during the periods of dissolution, where all creation withdraws into the primordial waters, symbolizes that while forms and manifestations may come and go, the underlying reality remains constant and eternal. Ananta's coils, ever-revolving yet ever-stable, represent the eternal recurrence of these cosmic cycles, reminding us that the end is merely a precursor to a new beginning.

The Symbolism of the Thousand Hoods

One of the most striking features of Ananta is his thousand hoods, often depicted as fanned out in a protective canopy over Lord Vishnu. These hoods are not just physical attributes but carry deep symbolic meanings. They represent the manifold aspects of the universe—time, space, knowledge, and the elements—all harmonized and balanced by the infinite nature of Ananta. The thousand hoods also signify the boundless knowledge and awareness that transcends ordinary comprehension. Each hood is said to contain an aspect of the universe's vast complexity, and yet, Ananta remains poised and tranquil, indicating that the infinite can contain and harmonize even the most chaotic and diverse aspects of existence.

Ananta's Role in Creation and Destruction

While Ananta is primarily associated with the preservation and continuity of the universe, his infinite nature also plays a crucial role in its creation and destruction. According to certain myths, at the beginning of creation, it is Shesha who carries the universe on his hoods, balancing it with perfect precision. As the cycles progress and dissolution becomes imminent, Ananta's coils contract, withdrawing the universe back into the cosmic ocean, where it awaits the next cycle of creation. This dynamic role underscores that Ananta is not merely a passive support but an active participant in the eternal rhythms of the cosmos. His actions are not driven by desire or will but by the inherent nature of infinity itself, which transcends and encompasses all dualities, including creation and destruction.

The Serpent of Knowledge and Wisdom

Ananta's association with serpents, creatures often linked to wisdom and esoteric knowledge, adds another layer to his symbolism. In many cultures, serpents are seen as guardians of sacred knowledge and keepers of secrets that lie beyond the grasp of the ordinary mind. Ananta, with his endless coils and serene demeanor, embodies the wisdom that lies at the heart of existence—the understanding that all phenomena are transient, yet the underlying reality is unchanging. This wisdom is not easily accessible; it requires one to go beyond the superficial layers of perception and to see with the eyes of the infinite. In this way, Ananta is not just the supporter of the universe but also the guardian of the deeper truths that sustain it.

Ananta in Devotion and Worship

In Hindu devotional practices, Ananta is venerated as the eternal servant of Vishnu, an embodiment of perfect devotion and surrender. This aspect of Ananta is celebrated in various rituals and prayers that honor his unwavering support for the divine order. The image of Vishnu reclining on Shesha is a common motif in temples and art, serving as a reminder of the cosmic balance maintained by the Infinite One. Devotees often invoke Ananta in prayers seeking stability, protection, and the strength to endure life's challenges, mirroring the serpent's role in upholding the universe through all its trials.

Ananta's significance extends beyond mere mythology; he is a profound symbol of the eternal, the unchanging essence that lies at the core of all existence. In a world characterized by impermanence and flux, Ananta stands as a testament to the enduring nature of the cosmos, a reminder that beneath the surface of change lies an unbreakable continuity. Through his endless coils, Ananta weaves the fabric of reality, ensuring that the dance of creation, preservation, and dissolution continues in an unbroken, infinite cycle.

Ananta, the Infinite One, is not just a figure in the cosmic narrative but a representation of the highest truths of existence. His presence in the cosmic ocean, as the steadfast supporter of the universe, serves as an eternal reminder that while forms may change and cycles may turn, the foundation of reality remains infinite, unchanging, and ever-present.

- The Ocean of Milk

In the vast expanse of Hindu mythology, the Ocean of Milk, known as Kshira Sagara, occupies a central place in the cosmic narrative. This celestial ocean is not just a mythical body of water but a profound symbol of the cosmic essence, a primordial sea from which the universe and all its wonders emerge. The Ocean of Milk is depicted as an endless, luminous expanse, shimmering with the purest, most nourishing substance in existence—milk, which itself is emblematic of sustenance, fertility, and the nurturing forces of the cosmos. In its depths lies the potential for all creation, the secret of immortality, and the very foundation of divine power. This ocean is most famously featured in the myth of the Samudra Manthan, the Churning of the Ocean, a pivotal event that highlights the eternal struggle between the forces of good and evil and the quest for Amrita, the nectar of immortality.

The Symbolism of the Ocean of Milk

The Ocean of Milk represents the primordial waters of creation, a concept that resonates across various cultures and mythologies. In Hindu cosmology, it stands as a metaphor for the unmanifest, undifferentiated state of existence that precedes creation. Just as milk is the source of nourishment and growth, Kshira Sagara symbolizes the boundless potential from which the universe emerges and into which it eventually dissolves. This ocean embodies the idea of cosmic fertility, where the raw materials of creation are suspended in a state of equilibrium, awaiting the divine impulse that sets the cycle of creation, preservation, and dissolution into motion.

Milk, as a substance, is universally recognized for its nourishing qualities. In the context of Kshira Sagara, it represents purity, abundance, and the sustaining force of the universe. It is from this ocean that the gods and demons seek to extract Amrita, the elixir of life, which underscores the notion that immortality and divine power lie within the essence of the cosmos itself. The Ocean of Milk is thus a reservoir of limitless possibilities, holding within its depths the secrets of life, energy, and the balance of the cosmos.

The Churning of the Ocean: Samudra Manthan

The most well-known narrative involving the Ocean of Milk is the story of Samudra Manthan, the churning of the ocean, a grand cosmic event that brought together the gods (Devas) and demons (Asuras) in a temporary alliance. This myth is a rich allegory for the human experience, encapsulating the struggles, desires, and aspirations that drive both celestial and mortal beings. The churning was initiated by the gods, who sought the elixir of immortality, Amrita, to regain their strength and supremacy over the demons. However, the task was monumental, and they required the cooperation of the Asuras, who were equally eager to obtain the nectar.

Mount Mandara was used as the churning rod, and the mighty serpent Vasuki served as the churning rope. Lord Vishnu, the preserver of the universe, took the form of a great tortoise, Kurma, to support the mountain on his back, preventing it from sinking into the ocean's depths. As the churning commenced, the Ocean of Milk began to yield a series of wondrous and terrifying substances, each symbolizing various aspects of existence.

The churning of Kshira Sagara is not merely a physical act but a profound representation of the cosmic process of transformation and creation. It symbolizes the tumultuous interplay of opposites—good and evil, light and darkness, order and chaos—that is necessary for the birth of new realities. The friction and cooperation between the Devas and Asuras reflect the dualities inherent in life, suggesting that creation often requires the blending of contradictory forces.

Emergence of Divine Treasures

As the churning continued, the Ocean of Milk began to produce an array of divine treasures and beings, each with significant symbolic meaning. Among these were:

- **Kamadhenu, the Divine Cow**: Symbolizing abundance, nourishment, and the endless generosity of nature, Kamadhenu emerged from the ocean as a source of all desires, embodying the nurturing aspect of the cosmos.

- **Airavata, the Celestial Elephant**: A symbol of royal power and wisdom, Airavata was claimed by Indra, the king of the gods, representing the divine authority and the strength to rule justly.

- **Kalpavriksha, the Wish-Fulfilling Tree**: Representing the fulfillment of all desires, this tree is a symbol of abundance and the potential for human aspirations to manifest into reality.

- **Goddess Lakshmi**: The goddess of wealth, prosperity, and beauty, Lakshmi's emergence signifies the prosperity that follows the harmonious balance of forces. She was immediately accepted by Lord Vishnu as his consort, highlighting the connection between sustenance and preservation.

- **Dhanvantari, the Divine Physician**: Emerging with the pot of Amrita, Dhanvantari symbolizes health, healing, and the knowledge of Ayurveda, the ancient science of life and longevity. The arrival of Dhanvantari underscores the idea that well-being is an integral part of cosmic balance.

Each of these treasures represents an essential aspect of existence, highlighting the Ocean of Milk as the source of all that is desirable and necessary for life. The churning process illustrates that it is through effort, struggle, and the interplay of diverse forces that the greatest gifts of existence are realized.

The Emergence of Halahala: The Poison of Negativity

However, not all that emerged from the churning was benevolent. One of the first substances to surface was Halahala, a deadly poison that threatened to destroy both gods and demons, as well as the entire universe. This moment in the myth highlights the inherent dangers and unpredictable outcomes of cosmic endeavors. The appearance of Halahala is symbolic of the negative forces that can arise even from the most noble of pursuits, representing the potential for harm that lies within the fabric of creation.

The gods, in their desperation, turned to Lord Shiva, the great destroyer and transformer. In a supreme act of self-sacrifice, Shiva drank the poison, holding it in his throat to prevent it from spreading, which turned his throat blue and earned him the name Neelkanth, the Blue-Throated One. This act not only saved the cosmos but also demonstrated the necessity of selflessness and sacrifice in the face of cosmic trials. Shiva's intervention emphasizes the importance of balance, showing that even amidst the pursuit of immortality and divine power, one must be willing to confront and neutralize the destructive forces that arise.

The Revelation of Amrita: The Nectar of Immortality

The climax of the churning was the emergence of Amrita, the nectar of immortality, held in a pot by Dhanvantari. This divine elixir, sought after by both Devas and Asuras, represents the ultimate goal of the cosmic struggle—the attainment of eternal life, divine wisdom, and unending bliss. However, the acquisition of Amrita was not straightforward. The Asuras, driven by their insatiable desire for power, immediately seized the nectar, threatening to keep it for themselves.

In response, Lord Vishnu, ever the preserver of cosmic order, assumed the form of Mohini, an enchanting female avatar, whose beauty and charm mesmerized the Asuras. Distracted by her allure, the Asuras willingly surrendered the pot of Amrita to Mohini, who then distributed it among the gods, ensuring that the forces of good triumphed. This episode highlights the role of divine intervention and the subtle interplay of wisdom, strategy, and illusion in the preservation of cosmic balance. Vishnu's intervention as Mohini underscores the idea that divine will and cleverness can overcome brute force and selfish ambition, guiding the cosmos towards harmony.

The Ocean of Milk as a Symbol of the Unconscious Mind

Beyond its cosmological significance, the Ocean of Milk can also be seen as a representation of the unconscious mind. Just as the churning of the ocean brings forth treasures and poison alike, the exploration of the unconscious mind can reveal profound insights, hidden potentials, and latent fears. The act of churning, then, becomes a metaphor for the spiritual journey, wherein one must confront both the divine and the demonic aspects of the self to achieve true understanding and enlightenment. The emergence of Amrita symbolizes the ultimate realization of self-awareness, a state of immortality and peace that transcends the dualities of existence.

The Ocean of Milk in Devotional Contexts

In Hindu devotional practice, the Ocean of Milk is not just a mythic backdrop but a profound symbol of the devotee's relationship with the divine. The cosmic ocean serves as a reminder of the limitless grace and potential that flows from the divine source. Rituals and prayers often invoke the image of the churning, encouraging devotees to engage in their own spiritual churning through practices such as meditation, prayer, and self-reflection. By invoking the Ocean of Milk, devotees seek to draw forth the divine treasures within themselves, aspiring to realize the Amrita of spiritual enlightenment and divine connection.

Temples dedicated to Vishnu, particularly those associated with his incarnations as Kurma or his role in the churning of the ocean, often feature elaborate depictions of the Samudra Manthan. These depictions serve not only as artistic and cultural touchstones but as spiritual reminders of the cosmic process that underlies all existence. They encourage devotees to reflect on the nature of their own struggles and the potential for divine intervention and grace in their lives.

Conclusion

The Ocean of Milk, with its endless expanse and profound symbolism, stands as one of the most evocative elements of Hindu mythology. It embodies the essence of creation, the unending potential of the cosmos, and the eternal quest for balance and immortality. Through the churning of Kshira Sagara, the narrative captures the complexities of existence, where the forces of good and evil, order and chaos, are in constant interplay. This myth serves as a powerful allegory for the human condition, reminding us that within the tumult of life, there lies the potential for the most divine of realizations. The Ocean of Milk is not just a cosmic sea but a reflection of the universal journey—an eternal dance of creation, preservation, and transformation, where the ultimate prize is the nectar of immortality, the realization of the divine within and beyond.

- ## Shesha's Role in the Churning of the Ocean

Shesha, the mighty serpent known as Ananta or the Infinite One, is a foundational figure in Hindu mythology, embodying stability, support, and the eternal nature of the universe. Often depicted as the bed on which Lord Vishnu rests, floating on the Ocean of Milk, Shesha's presence is not just symbolic of the foundational nature of existence but also of the intrinsic order underlying the cosmos. His role during the Churning of the Ocean (Samudra Manthan) is an often overlooked but essential aspect of this grand myth, highlighting the themes of balance, strength, and cosmic endurance.

The Cosmic Serpent: A Symbol of Eternity and Stability

Shesha's very name, meaning "remainder," speaks to his role as that which remains after the dissolution of the universe. As the serpent who bears the weight of all creation, Shesha is depicted with thousands of hoods, each crowned with a jewel, and a body that coils endlessly in cosmic loops. He represents the continuous cycle of time, the undying nature of reality, and the ever-present foundation upon which all existence rests. As the serpent who supports the universe, Shesha embodies the idea that even amidst chaos, there is an unshakeable base that maintains the order of the cosmos.

In the context of the Churning of the Ocean, Shesha's involvement is subtly interwoven into the narrative, providing a counterbalance to the more aggressive and dynamic forces at play. The churning of the Ocean of Milk is a cosmic event of immense magnitude, involving not only the gods (Devas) and demons (Asuras) but also various divine interventions. While the most visible forces in the churning are Vasuki, the churning rope, and Mount Mandara, the churning rod, Shesha's presence represents a deeper, underlying stability, ensuring that the cosmic endeavor does not collapse under its own magnitude.

The Churning of the Ocean: A Cosmic Endeavor

The Churning of the Ocean of Milk, or Samudra Manthan, is one of the most dramatic and symbolically rich myths in Hindu lore. In this story, the Devas and Asuras, driven by the desire to obtain Amrita, the nectar of immortality, join forces to churn the cosmic ocean. This endeavor required not only immense physical effort but also the balancing of cosmic forces, as the process threatened to destabilize the very fabric of the universe.

Mount Mandara was used as the churning rod, and the serpent Vasuki was coiled around the mountain as the churning rope. The gods pulled from one side, and the demons from the other, creating a powerful tension that symbolized the eternal struggle between opposing forces. Lord Vishnu, in his Kurma avatar, supported the mountain on his back, preventing it from sinking. In this dynamic and tension-filled event, Shesha's role, though not overtly highlighted, was crucial in maintaining the cosmic order that allowed the churning to proceed.

Shesha and Vasuki: Two Serpents, Different Roles

In the Samudra Manthan, the involvement of Vasuki as the churning rope is prominently depicted. Vasuki, with his immense length and strength, is stretched between the gods and demons, enduring the constant pull and friction of the churning. His participation is direct and involves enduring pain and struggle, as the constant tugging causes him to emit deadly fumes, representing the destructive aspect of the cosmic process.

Shesha, in contrast, plays a more subtle role. While Vasuki's efforts are visible and active, Shesha's presence is more symbolic, representing the underlying stability needed to keep the process in balance. Unlike Vasuki, who experiences the churning directly, Shesha embodies the broader support of the cosmos, upholding the forces at play without direct engagement. His role can be seen as the silent guardian, ensuring that the universal laws and equilibrium are maintained even as the forces of creation and destruction clash.

The Underlying Stability: Shesha's Invisible Support

Though Shesha does not physically participate in the churning, his cosmic function as the bedrock of existence underlies the entire event. The Ocean of Milk, representing the unmanifested potential of the universe, churns with the force of divine aspiration and demonic ambition. This process is fraught with instability, as Mount Mandara wobbles and sinks, and Vasuki struggles to endure the strain. Shesha's symbolic role is to provide the assurance that, no matter the chaos above, the fundamental stability of the universe remains intact.

This symbolic stability is crucial because it underscores the nature of cosmic balance. While Vishnu supports the mountain as Kurma, it is Shesha's cosmic essence that ensures the underlying forces remain aligned. He represents the eternal principles that do not waver, even when the visible universe is in flux. His presence is a reminder that behind every great cosmic endeavor lies a foundation that is both timeless and unchanging.

Shesha and Vishnu: The Eternal Connection

Shesha's deep connection with Vishnu is central to understanding his role in the churning. As the serpent upon which Vishnu rests, Shesha is intimately linked with the preserver of the universe. Vishnu's involvement in the Samudra Manthan is active—he takes the form of Kurma, calms Vasuki, and ultimately ensures the distribution of Amrita through his Mohini avatar. Shesha's role complements Vishnu's actions by providing the metaphysical foundation upon which Vishnu's interventions are grounded.

This connection between Vishnu and Shesha can be interpreted as the relationship between the visible actions of the divine and the unseen, eternal principles that support them. While Vishnu engages directly with the challenges of the universe, Shesha's presence is constant and unchanging, embodying the infinite potential that sustains Vishnu's efforts. In this sense, Shesha's role is not to engage directly but to provide the infinite canvas on which the divine drama unfolds.

The Lesson of Shesha's Role: Balance and Endurance

Shesha's involvement in the Churning of the Ocean serves as a profound reminder of the importance of stability, balance, and endurance in the cosmic order. While the narrative focus often lies on the more dynamic elements—the churning, the poison, the treasures, and the final acquisition of Amrita—Shesha's silent support is a critical element that allows these events to occur without the disintegration of the universe.

In many ways, Shesha's role mirrors the spiritual path. While one may engage in active practices like meditation, prayer, or service, it is the underlying stability of one's inner being that sustains these efforts. Shesha represents the foundation of faith, the unshakeable trust in the divine order, and the endurance required to navigate the tumultuous journey of life. His silent, supportive presence in the Churning of the Ocean teaches that not all contributions are visible or dramatic; some, like the presence of Shesha, are the quiet but crucial underpinnings that hold everything together.

Shesha in Devotional and Philosophical Contexts

In devotional contexts, Shesha's role in the Churning of the Ocean can be viewed as a metaphor for the inner support that the divine provides to all beings. Just as Shesha upholds the cosmos, so too does the divine uphold the individual soul, offering stability amidst the churning forces of life's challenges. Devotees may invoke Shesha as a symbol of strength and endurance, seeking his blessing to maintain their spiritual composure in times of turmoil.

Philosophically, Shesha embodies the concept of the substratum of existence—the idea that beneath all change and transformation, there is an unchanging reality. This aligns with the Vedantic notion of Brahman, the ultimate, unchanging reality that underlies the universe. Shesha, as the cosmic serpent, is a tangible representation of this principle, demonstrating that no matter the upheaval on the surface, the foundation remains steady.

Shesha's Role in the Broader Cosmic Framework

The Churning of the Ocean is but one episode in the vast tapestry of Hindu mythology, but it encapsulates many key themes of cosmic balance, the struggle between good and evil, and the pursuit of immortality. Shesha's role, though often understated, serves as a reminder of the importance of foundational principles in any endeavor. Whether in the cosmic scale of the universe or the personal journey of the soul, Shesha's silent support is a metaphor for the essential, enduring truths that sustain all of existence.

In the grand narrative of the Churning of the Ocean, Shesha stands as a silent sentinel, a guardian of cosmic order whose presence ensures that the process of creation and transformation can proceed without unraveling the fabric of reality. His role is a testament to the power of quiet endurance and the necessity of an unshakeable foundation in the face of the universe's ever-changing dance. Through Shesha, the myth of Samudra Manthan teaches that while the forces of creation may churn and clash, there is always an underlying force of stability, ensuring that the cosmos remains whole and harmonious.

Chapter 3: Shesha as Vishnu's Throne

- ## The Divine Throne

Shesha, the mighty cosmic serpent, occupies a unique and exalted position in Hindu mythology as the divine throne of Lord Vishnu. Often depicted as a multi-headed serpent with thousands of hoods, Shesha serves as the resting place for Vishnu, who reclines on Shesha's coils upon the Ocean of Milk, in a state of eternal repose. This image, profoundly rich in symbolism, transcends mere artistic representation to encapsulate some of the deepest philosophical and metaphysical concepts in Hinduism. The portrayal of Shesha as Vishnu's throne signifies the unbreakable connection between the divine and the eternal, the balance of cosmic forces, and the profound tranquility that underlies the workings of the universe.

Shesha and Vishnu: The Eternal Bond

The relationship between Shesha and Vishnu is one of the most enduring symbols of cosmic order and harmony. Vishnu, the preserver of the universe, represents the sustaining force that maintains creation in a state of balance. He embodies compassion, order, and the divine will that ensures the universe functions as it should. Shesha, on the other hand, represents the eternal and infinite nature of time and space, the unending cycles of creation, preservation, and dissolution. Together, they form a partnership that is both dynamic and serene, illustrating the balance between action and stillness, between the manifest and the unmanifest.

Shesha's position as Vishnu's throne goes beyond the physical; it is a manifestation of the philosophical idea that the divine rests upon the foundation of the eternal. Vishnu's repose on Shesha is not mere relaxation but a profound state of cosmic meditation (yoga nidra), where the universe exists in a state of potential. In this meditative state, Vishnu is constantly aware and ready to act when the time comes to restore order in the cosmos, while Shesha remains the silent, unwavering support, embodying the endless nature of time and existence.

The Symbolism of the Divine Throne

The imagery of Vishnu reclining on Shesha carries deep symbolism. Shesha's countless hoods, often depicted adorned with jewels and spread wide like an umbrella over Vishnu, represent the innumerable facets of the cosmos, each hood symbolizing an aspect of the universe. The multi-headed serpent's ability to balance all of these aspects reflects the cosmic balance that is essential to the stability of creation. The jewel-encrusted hoods also symbolize wisdom, protection, and the light of knowledge that illuminates the path of dharma.

In Hindu iconography, the ocean upon which Vishnu rests represents the Kshira Sagara, the Ocean of Milk, which symbolizes the primordial waters of creation, the vast, unmanifest potential from which the universe arises. Vishnu's resting position on Shesha amidst these waters signifies the unmanifest state of the cosmos, where all creation is held in balance, awaiting the divine impulse that will set the cycle of time into motion. This imagery encapsulates the essence of Vishnu's role as the preserver; even in stillness, he is the fulcrum around which the universe turns, with Shesha as his steadfast foundation.

Shesha's form as an endless serpent also symbolizes the cyclical nature of time—without beginning or end. This aligns with the Hindu concept of kala (time), which is both infinite and cyclical. The coils of Shesha represent the cycles of time, the yugas, and the eternal nature of cosmic law (rita). As Vishnu's throne, Shesha signifies that the divine presence is not bound by time but rather resides eternally beyond it, observing and influencing the unfolding of cosmic events.

The Throne as a Metaphor for Divine Governance

The concept of a throne traditionally symbolizes authority, governance, and the seat of power. In the case of Vishnu and Shesha, this symbolism takes on a cosmic dimension. Shesha as Vishnu's throne is not just a seat but a living entity that participates in the divine governance of the universe. Unlike a static, inanimate throne, Shesha is dynamic, alive, and conscious. He embodies the principles that uphold the cosmos: endurance, stability, and the continuity of time.

In this metaphor, Vishnu's reclining posture is not one of inactivity but of poised readiness. As the preserver, Vishnu governs the universe with an unassuming grace, maintaining order not through force but through the subtle balance of dharma (righteousness) and compassion. Shesha, as his throne, represents the underlying principles that make this governance possible. He is the silent force that sustains the universe's framework, allowing Vishnu to execute his role as the cosmic preserver.

Furthermore, the throne of Shesha is a reminder of the humility inherent in divine power. Shesha's posture—subservient, supportive, and ever-present—illustrates the ideal of selfless service. Despite his immense power and status as a primordial being, Shesha willingly submits to the role of Vishnu's bed, highlighting the importance of duty and service in the cosmic order. This humility is not weakness but strength, a reflection of the deeper understanding that true power lies in upholding and supporting the divine purpose.

Shesha's Role in Vishnu's Cosmic Repose

The depiction of Vishnu in a state of cosmic repose (yoga nidra) upon Shesha's coils is a powerful representation of the dynamic stillness at the heart of the universe. In this state, Vishnu is not asleep in the ordinary sense but is engaged in a deep meditative state that transcends time and space. This meditation is a preparatory phase, a gathering of divine energy that precedes the acts of creation, preservation, and dissolution. Shesha's role in this is crucial, as he provides the foundation upon which Vishnu can remain in this meditative state, undisturbed by the external chaos of the manifest universe.

Shesha's support extends beyond the physical; he represents the unwavering cosmic principles that allow Vishnu's meditation to endure. In this sense, Shesha can be seen as the guardian of cosmic order, ensuring that the divine rest of Vishnu is not disturbed, allowing the universe to remain in balance. This state of repose is essential to the maintenance of the cosmos; it is a period of reflection and potential, where the seeds of future actions are sown.

The image of Shesha and Vishnu during this repose serves as a powerful metaphor for the cycles of rest and activity that are inherent in all aspects of existence. Just as the universe must undergo periods of quiescence before bursts of creation, so too must individuals recognize the importance of rest and reflection in their own lives. Shesha's support of Vishnu's repose reminds us that stillness is not inactivity but a necessary precursor to meaningful action.

The Divine Throne and the Concept of Cosmic Balance

The relationship between Shesha and Vishnu also illustrates the concept of cosmic balance, a central theme in Hindu philosophy. This balance is not a static state but a dynamic equilibrium, constantly maintained through the interplay of various forces. Shesha, as the embodiment of time and the eternal cycles, represents one aspect of this balance, while Vishnu, as the preserver, represents the force that maintains order within these cycles.

Shesha's presence as the throne upon which Vishnu rests symbolizes the necessary support structure that allows balance to be maintained. This support is not passive; it is an active engagement with the forces of the cosmos, an assurance that despite the ceaseless churn of time, the foundational principles of existence remain intact. In this way, Shesha's role as Vishnu's throne is a powerful reminder that behind every act of preservation, there must be an enduring foundation, a base upon which all else can rely.

The throne of Shesha also symbolizes the idea that divine governance is not arbitrary but is grounded in eternal laws and principles. Just as Shesha supports Vishnu, these principles support the divine actions that sustain the universe. This relationship underscores the importance of dharma, the cosmic law that governs all actions and ensures the stability of creation. In the broader cosmic framework, Shesha's role as the divine throne illustrates that true power is rooted in adherence to these universal principles, and that all actions, even those of the gods, must align with this fundamental order.

The Throne in Devotional Contexts

In devotional contexts, the image of Shesha as Vishnu's throne is often invoked as a symbol of divine support and protection. Devotees may meditate on this image as a reminder of the divine presence that underlies all aspects of life. Shesha's supportive role inspires believers to seek a similar foundation in their own spiritual practice—a steadfastness and resilience that can weather the challenges of life.

The throne of Shesha is also a metaphor for the soul's relationship with the divine. Just as Shesha supports Vishnu, so too does the devotee strive to support the divine purpose through their actions and intentions. This image serves as a call to humility and service, encouraging devotees to align their lives with the divine will and to seek the stability and peace that comes from resting in the presence of the divine.

In rituals and temple worship, Shesha's image is often present in the form of serpentine iconography, reminding worshippers of the eternal support that sustains the cosmos. The coils of Shesha, encircling the deity, serve as a protective barrier, symbolizing the divine embrace that shields the universe from chaos. This protective aspect of Shesha is a source of comfort and reassurance, illustrating that no matter how turbulent the outer world may be, the inner foundation remains unshaken.

Shesha and the Eternal Witness

As Vishnu reclines on Shesha, he gazes out over the Ocean of Milk, the vast expanse of unmanifest potential. This gaze is often interpreted as the divine vision that encompasses all of creation, a reminder that the divine is both within and beyond the manifest world. Shesha, as the divine throne, shares in this vision, acting as the eternal witness to the unfolding of the cosmos.

Shesha's role as the eternal witness is a profound aspect of his identity. Unlike the active roles played by other deities, Shesha's role is one of observation and support, embodying the principle that there is a silent, watchful presence behind all of existence. This presence is not indifferent but is deeply engaged with the cosmos, maintaining the balance and order that allows life to flourish.

In this sense, Shesha's role as the divine throne is a call to mindfulness and awareness. Just as Shesha witnesses the universe from his position beneath Vishnu, so too are individuals encouraged to adopt a stance of watchfulness in their own lives. This watchfulness is not passive; it is a vigilant awareness that sees beyond the surface of things, recognizing the deeper patterns and principles at play.

Conclusion: The Timeless Throne of Shesha

Shesha, as the divine throne of Vishnu, represents one of the most enduring and powerful symbols in Hindu mythology. His role transcends the physical to encompass the deepest philosophical and metaphysical principles, illustrating the eternal nature of time, the balance of cosmic forces, and the foundational support that sustains the universe. As the throne of Vishnu, Shesha embodies the principles of endurance, humility, and service, offering a profound lesson in the importance of these qualities in the divine order.

Through the image of Vishnu resting on Shesha, we are reminded of the interconnectedness of all things, the delicate balance that maintains the cosmos, and the eternal principles that underlie all existence. Shesha's role as the divine throne is not just a support for the divine but a vital participant in the cosmic drama, illustrating that true power lies not in domination but in the humble, steadfast support of the greater good. In this, Shesha serves as an eternal reminder of the beauty and profundity of the divine order, and the enduring presence of the sacred in every aspect of the universe.

- The Symbolic Interpretation

In the vast and intricate tapestry of Hindu mythology, Shesha, the cosmic serpent, stands out not just as a mighty creature of immense power but as a profound symbol deeply woven into the philosophical fabric of the cosmos. Depicted as an infinite serpent with thousands of hoods, each adorned with glowing jewels and spreading out like a divine canopy, Shesha transcends his physical form to embody the timeless principles of creation, preservation, and the cyclical nature of existence. His presence, particularly as the eternal throne of Lord Vishnu, serves as a multi-layered symbol representing the vast and complex dynamics of the universe. In exploring the symbolic interpretation of Shesha, we delve into the deeper meanings that his imagery holds, unveiling insights into the nature of the cosmos, the human condition, and the eternal dance of the divine forces.

The Infinite Serpent: A Symbol of Eternity and Time

At the heart of Shesha's symbolism is his portrayal as an endless serpent, an unbroken loop without beginning or end. This imagery is a powerful representation of eternity, the concept of time that stretches infinitely in both directions—past and future—without ever reaching a point of cessation. In Hindu thought, time (kala) is cyclical rather than linear, marked by an unending succession of cycles, or yugas, that repeat in perpetuity. Shesha, as the embodiment of this endless cycle, reflects the nature of the universe itself: ever-repeating, ever-renewing, and eternally enduring. His coiled form represents the cycles of time and existence, encapsulating the idea that the universe is in a constant state of flux, yet anchored in an unchanging reality.

Shesha's countless hoods, each representing different facets of time and space, further emphasize the multiplicity and diversity inherent in the cosmos. These hoods are not merely protective but also indicative of the many layers and dimensions of reality, suggesting that the universe is composed of a vast array of interlocking systems, each playing its part in the grand cosmic order. The serpent's coiling nature also signifies the spirals of time—each coil a representation of a different epoch or era, all contained within the infinite expanse of Shesha's form. This imagery invites contemplation on the nature of existence and the eternal journey of the soul through the cycles of birth, death, and rebirth, a journey that Shesha silently witnesses and supports.

Shesha as the Cosmic Bed: Balance and Stability

In his role as the divine throne for Vishnu, Shesha is a symbol of stability amidst the ever-changing universe. Vishnu, the preserver, reclines upon Shesha in a state of cosmic meditation, maintaining the balance of the universe even in repose. This act symbolizes the underlying stability that allows the cosmos to function harmoniously, despite the constant motion and change that characterize existence. Shesha's unwavering presence beneath Vishnu represents the eternal support structure that upholds the universe, a foundation that is both resilient and flexible, capable of accommodating the dynamic forces of creation, preservation, and destruction.

Shesha's symbolism extends beyond mere physical support; he embodies the concept of dharma, the cosmic law that governs the universe. In this role, Shesha is a metaphor for the underlying principles that sustain reality—principles that are inviolable and constant, yet flexible enough to adapt to the unfolding of cosmic events. Just as Shesha supports Vishnu without faltering, dharma upholds the universe, ensuring that every action, every force, and every being has a place and purpose within the grand scheme of existence.

This symbolism of balance is also evident in the interplay between Shesha and Vishnu. While Vishnu represents the active force of preservation, Shesha symbolizes the passive, yet essential, stability that underlies this action. Together, they illustrate the dual nature of existence: the active and the passive, the manifest and the unmanifest, the seen and the unseen. This duality is at the core of Hindu philosophy, where the balance between opposing forces—light and darkness, creation and destruction, action and stillness—is necessary for the maintenance of cosmic harmony.

The Thousand Hoods: Wisdom, Protection, and Multiplicity

Shesha's depiction with a thousand hoods, each crowned with a jewel that radiates divine light, is another layer of symbolism rich with meaning. These hoods are not only protective but also represent the myriad aspects of wisdom and consciousness that pervade the universe. The jewels symbolize enlightenment and the light of knowledge that dispels the darkness of ignorance. In this way, Shesha's hoods can be seen as a metaphor for the vast, interconnected web of understanding that sustains the cosmos, suggesting that wisdom is not singular but multifaceted, encompassing countless perspectives and truths.

Each of Shesha's hoods also represents a different aspect of reality, underscoring the Hindu belief in the multiplicity of existence. Just as Shesha's hoods spread out to form a canopy over Vishnu, the universe itself is composed of countless dimensions and planes of existence, all interconnected and interdependent. This symbolism aligns with the Vedic concept of Indra's Net, a metaphor used to describe the interconnectedness of all things, where each jewel in the net reflects all others, illustrating the infinite interrelationship of the universe. Shesha, as the multi-hooded serpent, serves as a living embodiment of this principle, reminding us that all aspects of existence are interconnected, and that the divine is present in all things.

Moreover, the protective nature of Shesha's hoods speaks to his role as a guardian of cosmic order. By shielding Vishnu, Shesha symbolizes the protective force that guards the universe against chaos and dissolution. This protective role is not one of aggression but of passive strength, demonstrating that true power lies in the ability to support and preserve rather than to dominate or control. Shesha's gentle yet firm presence underscores the importance of nurturing and sustaining the divine balance, an essential aspect of his symbolic interpretation.

Shesha and the Cosmic Ocean: The Unmanifest Potential

Shesha's association with the Ocean of Milk, upon which Vishnu reclines, adds yet another layer to his symbolic significance. The ocean represents the unmanifest potential of the universe, the primordial waters from which all creation arises. In Hindu cosmology, these waters are the source of all life, the fertile ground of existence, and the embodiment of the unformed possibilities that lie at the heart of the cosmos. Shesha's presence in this ocean signifies his connection to the unmanifest, the state of being that precedes creation.

This symbolism highlights Shesha's role as a bridge between the manifest and the unmanifest, the known and the unknown. As the throne of Vishnu, Shesha is the medium through which the divine engages with the potential of creation, resting upon the waters of the unmanifest and drawing forth the energy needed to sustain the cosmos. This interplay between Shesha, Vishnu, and the Ocean of Milk is a powerful reminder of the interdependence of all things, the delicate balance between potential and reality, and the continuous flow of energy that sustains life.

Shesha's association with the ocean also points to the idea of surrender and acceptance. Just as the ocean embraces all rivers, accepting their flow without resistance, Shesha represents the principle of surrender to the divine will, the acceptance of one's role within the cosmic order. This acceptance is not passive resignation but an active engagement with the divine purpose, a recognition that every being, every force, and every element has its place and function within the greater whole.

Shesha as the Embodiment of Dharma and Service

One of the most profound aspects of Shesha's symbolism is his embodiment of dharma, the cosmic order that governs the universe. In his role as Vishnu's throne, Shesha is a living representation of the principles of duty, service, and humility. Despite his immense power and status as a primordial being, Shesha willingly assumes the role of support and service, illustrating the importance of selflessness in the cosmic order. This selflessness is not a denial of self but an acknowledgment of the greater purpose that guides all actions.

Shesha's example teaches that true dharma lies not in seeking personal glory or power but in fulfilling one's role within the divine plan. His willingness to serve Vishnu, to support the divine without question or hesitation, exemplifies the ideal of surrender to the divine will. This surrender is not a loss of agency but a harmonious alignment with the cosmic order, a recognition that one's true purpose is found in service to the greater good.

In this context, Shesha's symbolism extends beyond the cosmic to the personal, offering a model for individuals to emulate in their own lives. Just as Shesha supports Vishnu, so too are we called to support the divine purpose in our actions, to live in accordance with dharma, and to embrace our roles within the larger tapestry of existence. This embrace of dharma is a path to fulfillment and harmony, a way of living that brings one into alignment with the eternal principles that sustain the universe.

Shesha and the Cycle of Creation, Preservation, and Destruction

Shesha's symbolism also encompasses the cyclical nature of creation, preservation, and destruction—key concepts in Hindu cosmology. As the eternal serpent, Shesha represents the unbroken continuity of these cycles, the endless loop of time that encompasses all of existence. His role as the bed of Vishnu, the preserver, places him at the center of the cosmic cycle, supporting the force that maintains the balance between creation and destruction.

In Hindu mythology, the universe is continually created, preserved, and destroyed in an endless cycle, each phase necessary for the renewal of life. Shesha's presence at the heart of this cycle symbolizes the eternal nature of these processes, reminding us that creation and destruction are not opposing forces but complementary aspects of a greater whole. Just as Vishnu preserves the universe, Brahma creates it, and Shiva destroys it, Shesha provides the stable foundation upon which these forces act, ensuring that the cycle continues unbroken.

This cyclical nature is also reflected in the image of Shesha shedding his skin, a process that symbolizes renewal and transformation. Just as the serpent sheds its old skin to reveal a fresh layer beneath, so too does the universe undergo continual cycles of death and rebirth, each shedding of the old making way for the new. Shesha's role in this process is one of quiet endurance, a reminder that amidst the constant change of the cosmos, there is a steady, unchanging presence that endures through all transformations.

The Eternal Witness: Shesha's Role as the Observer

Finally, Shesha's role as the eternal throne of Vishnu also positions him as a witness to the unfolding of the cosmos. In this role, Shesha is not an active participant in the events of the universe but a silent observer, a reminder that there is value in stillness and observation. This aspect of Shesha's symbolism speaks to the importance of mindfulness and awareness, the ability to observe without becoming entangled, to witness without judgment or attachment.

In the broader context of Hindu philosophy, this role of the witness is akin to the concept of the Atman, the true self that observes all without being affected by the fluctuations of the mind or the world. Just as Shesha observes the cosmic play from his position beneath Vishnu, so too does the Atman observe the play of life, detached yet fully engaged. This witnessing is not passive but a profound form of engagement, one that sees the truth of things without becoming lost in the illusion of separation.

Through Shesha, we are reminded that there is a part of us that is eternal and unchanging, a presence that watches over the flow of life with calm and clarity. This presence is not separate from the world but intimately connected to it, just as Shesha is both within the cosmos and beyond it. In embracing the role of the witness, we align ourselves with the eternal principles that Shesha embodies, finding peace in the knowledge that beneath the surface of all things lies an unchanging reality.

Conclusion: The Profound Symbolism of Shesha

Shesha, as the cosmic serpent and divine throne of Vishnu, is far more than a mythical creature; he is a living symbol of the eternal principles that govern the universe. Through his infinite form, his support of Vishnu, and his role as a witness to the cosmic play, Shesha embodies the concepts of eternity, stability, balance, and service. His presence is a reminder of the interconnectedness of all things, the cyclical nature of existence, and the enduring truth that underlies all creation.

In the symbolism of Shesha, we find a reflection of the deepest truths of Hindu philosophy: that the universe is a vast, interconnected web of existence, that time is a continuous cycle of renewal, and that true power lies in the humble support of the divine order. Shesha's role as the divine throne is not just a position of service but a profound expression of the principles that sustain the cosmos, offering a model of endurance, humility, and wisdom that resonates through the ages.

As we contemplate the image of Shesha, we are invited to look beyond the surface of things, to see the deeper patterns that shape reality, and to embrace our own roles within the grand tapestry of existence. In doing so, we honor the timeless presence of Shesha, the eternal witness and supporter of the divine, and find our place within the ever-unfolding drama of the cosmos.

• Shesha as the Preserver of Dharma

In the vast and intricate mythology of Hinduism, Shesha, the mighty serpent with a thousand hoods, stands as one of the most revered and profound symbols of cosmic balance and order. Known primarily as the eternal throne of Lord Vishnu, Shesha transcends his physical form to embody deeper philosophical principles, chief among them the preservation of Dharma. Dharma, in Hindu philosophy, represents the universal law, righteousness, and the moral order that sustains the cosmos and guides all beings. As the Preserver of Dharma, Shesha plays a critical role in maintaining the balance of the universe, subtly upholding the forces that govern creation, preservation, and destruction. To fully appreciate Shesha's significance in this regard, it is essential to delve into the layers of symbolism and the narratives that portray him as the silent yet steadfast guardian of cosmic order.

The Concept of Dharma: The Pillar of Existence

Before exploring Shesha's role in preserving Dharma, it is vital to understand what Dharma represents within the context of Hindu thought. Dharma is more than just righteousness or moral law; it is the foundational principle that underpins the functioning of the universe. It encompasses the duties, rights, laws, conduct, virtues, and the way of life that align with the order of the cosmos. Dharma is the path of truth, the principle of balance, and the force that keeps the world in harmony. In the grand cosmic scheme, Dharma ensures that every entity, from the smallest grain of sand to the vast expanses of galaxies, operates in accordance with its inherent nature and purpose.

Dharma is not static; it adapts to the context of time, place, and circumstance, yet remains rooted in the eternal truths that transcend temporal fluctuations. It governs the cycles of birth, life, and death, guiding the moral compass of individuals and the collective evolution of societies. In this light, Dharma is seen as both a personal duty and a cosmic order, interlinking the microcosm of individual actions with the macrocosm of universal laws. It is within this vast framework of Dharma that Shesha's role as a preserver is illuminated, portraying him not merely as a passive supporter of Vishnu but as an active upholder of the cosmic order.

Shesha and Vishnu: The Symbiosis of Preservation

Shesha's intimate association with Vishnu, the Preserver among the Trimurti, is a pivotal aspect of his role as the preserver of Dharma. Vishnu, who embodies the principle of sustenance and maintenance, relies on Shesha as his eternal throne, resting upon the serpent's coils amidst the Ocean of Milk. This imagery is deeply symbolic, depicting the symbiotic relationship between Vishnu and Shesha. While Vishnu actively engages in the preservation of the universe, manifesting in various avatars to restore balance and order, Shesha serves as the passive yet essential foundation that upholds Vishnu's actions. Shesha's presence beneath Vishnu signifies the steady, unyielding support of Dharma, a silent force that ensures the preservation of cosmic balance.

In this context, Shesha can be seen as the underlying principle that sustains the universe, providing the necessary stability for Vishnu's acts of preservation. Just as a throne supports a king, allowing him to govern with authority and wisdom, Shesha's coils provide the platform upon which Vishnu performs his divine duties. This support is not merely physical but metaphysical, representing the foundation of Dharma upon which the universe rests. Shesha's unwavering presence symbolizes the unbroken continuity of Dharma, the eternal law that persists through all cycles of time, ensuring that the forces of creation, preservation, and destruction remain in harmony.

The Thousand Hoods: Guardianship and Vigilance

Shesha's thousand hoods, each crowned with a radiant jewel, are more than a display of his grandeur; they symbolize his vigilance and guardianship over the cosmos. These hoods, spreading out like a protective canopy over Vishnu, represent the myriad aspects of Dharma that govern the universe. Each hood can be seen as a facet of Dharma, reflecting different principles such as truth, justice, duty, and compassion, all of which are essential to maintaining the cosmic order. Shesha's vigilant stance, with his eyes ever-watchful, conveys his role as the guardian of these principles, ensuring that they are upheld across the vast expanse of existence.

In mythological narratives, Shesha is often depicted as maintaining a meditative state, his focus unwavering even amidst the tumult of cosmic events. This meditative vigilance is a powerful metaphor for the constancy of Dharma, which remains steadfast even in the face of chaos and disorder. Shesha's unblinking eyes symbolize the unceasing watchfulness required to preserve balance, a reminder that the preservation of Dharma is not a passive act but one that demands continuous awareness and engagement. Through this imagery, Shesha embodies the ideal of dharma-preservation: an active, conscious effort to uphold the moral and cosmic order, ever-mindful of the delicate balance that sustains life.

Shesha and the Cosmic Ocean: Sustaining the Unmanifest

The Ocean of Milk, upon which Vishnu reclines on Shesha, represents the unmanifest potential of the universe, the primordial waters from which all creation emerges. This ocean is a symbol of the unformed, undifferentiated state of existence, the vast potential that lies at the heart of the cosmos. In his role as the bed of Vishnu, Shesha acts as the bridge between the unmanifest and the manifest, supporting the forces that bring order and form to the formless expanse of potential. This act of support is not just about physical sustenance but represents the maintenance of the cosmic equilibrium, the delicate balance between chaos and order that allows the universe to function harmoniously.

Shesha's presence in the Ocean of Milk also speaks to his role in sustaining the primordial principles that govern creation. The ocean itself is a representation of the infinite possibilities that exist before the act of creation, a state of pure potential that is held in check by the principles of Dharma. Shesha, as the preserver of Dharma, ensures that this potential is harnessed in accordance with the cosmic order, allowing creation to unfold in a manner that maintains balance and harmony. This process of sustaining the unmanifest potential reflects Shesha's deeper role as a stabilizing force within the universe, one that upholds the principles of Dharma even before they manifest in the physical world.

The Serpent's Coils: The Cyclical Nature of Dharma

Shesha's coiled form is a potent symbol of the cyclical nature of existence, reflecting the continuous cycles of creation, preservation, and destruction that define the universe. In Hindu cosmology, these cycles are governed by the principles of Dharma, which ensure that each phase of the cycle unfolds in accordance with the cosmic order. Shesha's coils, winding endlessly around themselves, represent the unbroken continuity of these cycles, a reminder that Dharma is not a fixed state but a dynamic force that adapts to the changing circumstances of time and space.

Each coil of Shesha can be seen as a distinct cycle within the broader flow of existence, whether it be the cycles of day and night, the seasons, or the yugas that define cosmic time. These cycles are not random but are governed by the principles of Dharma, which maintain the balance between the forces of creation and destruction. Shesha, as the preserver of Dharma, embodies the stability that allows these cycles to continue without interruption, ensuring that the universe remains in a state of perpetual renewal. His coiled form serves as a visual metaphor for the cyclical nature of Dharma, reminding us that while the forms of existence may change, the underlying principles remain constant.

Shesha's Role in Cosmic Justice: The Enforcer of Rta

In Vedic tradition, Rta is the principle of cosmic order that governs the universe, a precursor to the concept of Dharma. Rta is the natural order that ensures the regularity of the seasons, the movements of the celestial bodies, and the moral order of the world. As the preserver of Dharma, Shesha is intimately connected to the principle of Rta, serving as an enforcer of this cosmic order. His presence beneath Vishnu symbolizes the foundation of Rta, the unchanging reality that supports the universe's structure and ensures that all things operate in accordance with their true nature.

Shesha's association with Rta extends to his role as a guardian of cosmic justice. In Hindu mythology, justice is not merely about punishment or reward but about restoring balance and harmony. Shesha's vigilant presence serves as a reminder that every action, whether by gods, humans, or demons, must align with the cosmic order, and any deviation from this path disrupts the balance of the universe. As the preserver of Dharma, Shesha ensures that the scales of cosmic justice are balanced, maintaining the equilibrium that allows life to flourish.

This aspect of Shesha's role is particularly evident in his association with Vishnu's avatars, many of whom descend to the earthly realm to restore Dharma when it is threatened. While Vishnu takes active forms to combat adharma, Shesha's presence remains a constant, an ever-watchful guardian that upholds the principles of Rta behind the scenes. Through this partnership, Shesha embodies the passive aspect of justice, the silent force that ensures the continuity of order even as the avatars actively engage with the forces of chaos.

The Inner Journey: Shesha as the Guide to Self-Dharma

While Shesha's role as the preserver of cosmic Dharma is profound, his symbolism also extends to the personal realm, offering insights into the concept of self-Dharma or svadharma. In Hindu philosophy, svadharma refers to an individual's personal duty, the unique path that each person must follow in accordance with their nature, talents, and circumstances. Shesha's steady support of Vishnu serves as a metaphor for the importance of aligning oneself with one's true purpose, acting as a reminder that fulfilling one's svadharma is essential to maintaining personal balance and harmony.

In this light, Shesha's vigilance and stability can be seen as guiding principles for the inner journey of self-discovery and self-fulfillment. His unwavering presence symbolizes the importance of staying true to one's path, even amidst the challenges and uncertainties of life. Just as Shesha remains steadfast beneath Vishnu, supporting the divine mission, so too must individuals remain grounded in their svadharma, upholding their personal duties with integrity and commitment. Shesha's role as the preserver of Dharma thus extends beyond the cosmic order to encompass the inner order of the self, offering a model of how to live in harmony with one's true nature.

Conclusion: Shesha, the Silent Guardian of Order

Shesha, the eternal serpent, is far more than a mythical creature; he is a profound symbol of the forces that sustain the universe. As the preserver of Dharma, Shesha embodies the principles of balance, vigilance, and stability that are essential to maintaining cosmic order. Through his association with Vishnu, his coiled form, and his vigilant guardianship, Shesha represents the continuity of Dharma, the unbroken thread that weaves through the fabric of existence, ensuring that all things operate in harmony with their true nature.

Shesha's symbolism serves as a powerful reminder of the interconnectedness of all things, the cyclical nature of life, and the importance of aligning oneself with the principles of Dharma. His presence beneath Vishnu is not just a position of support but a profound expression of the enduring truths that sustain the cosmos. In Shesha, we find a model of how to uphold order in both the outer world and the inner self, embracing the role of the preserver in our own lives and finding peace in the knowledge that we are part of a greater, unchanging reality.

Through the lens of Shesha's symbolism, we are invited to reflect on our own roles within the grand tapestry of existence, to recognize the importance of balance and vigilance in our pursuit of Dharma, and to find strength in the silent, steadfast presence that underlies all of creation. In honoring Shesha, we honor the eternal principles that guide us, finding our place within the cosmic order and embracing the timeless dance of life with wisdom, humility, and grace.

Chapter 4: Shesha and the Cycle of Time

- The Endless Cycles of Yugas

In the grand tapestry of Hindu cosmology, the concept of time is not linear, as in many Western traditions, but cyclical. This cyclicality is an essential aspect of the universe's eternal rhythm, embodied by the serpent Shesha, who represents cosmic balance and the unceasing flow of time. Central to this understanding are the Yugas, the four ages that make up the cosmic cycle, each of which reflects a different stage in the moral and spiritual evolution—or devolution—of the universe. These Yugas, or epochs, recur in an unbroken cycle, illustrating the eternal, recurring nature of creation, destruction, and rebirth.

The four Yugas—Satya Yuga, Treta Yuga, Dvapara Yuga, and Kali Yuga—progress in a descending order of moral righteousness and harmony. Each successive age experiences a gradual decline in dharma, or righteousness, culminating in the most degenerate state during the Kali Yuga, after which the cycle begins anew. The understanding of the Yugas is intricately connected to Shesha, who is often depicted supporting the universe, embodying the eternal, unyielding nature of cosmic time and the cyclical existence of all life.

The Concept of Yugas

In Hindu cosmology, time is divided into vast units that are incomprehensible from a human perspective, with each cycle of Yugas encompassing millions of human years. The four Yugas together form a Mahayuga, a great age. After one Mahayuga is completed, the cycle begins again, much like the rising and setting of the sun, a reflection of the universe's cyclical nature.

The duration of the four Yugas follows a proportional decline in time and moral virtue:

- **Satya Yuga** (the age of truth) lasts 1,728,000 human years and is characterized by perfect harmony and righteousness. Dharma, or virtue, stands firmly on four legs, and human beings live in perfect accord with divine principles.

- **Treta Yuga** lasts 1,296,000 human years and sees a slight decline in dharma, as it now stands on three legs. This is the age of the Ramayana and other epic narratives, where gods and humans interact more closely, yet challenges to righteousness begin to arise.

- **Dvapara Yuga** lasts 864,000 years, with dharma standing on two legs. This age is marked by strife, moral ambiguity, and the waning of spiritual power. The Mahabharata, the great epic, takes place in this era, symbolizing the growing tension between good and evil.

- **Kali Yuga** is the shortest, lasting 432,000 years, but it is the age of greatest darkness and moral corruption. Dharma now stands on one leg, indicating the extreme instability and chaos of this time. Kali Yuga, the age in which we currently exist, is marked by ignorance, materialism, and the breakdown of societal and spiritual order.

At the end of the Kali Yuga, the cycle resets, beginning again with Satya Yuga in a process known as *pralaya*, or dissolution, when the universe is destroyed and reborn.

Shesha: The Cosmic Serpent and Time's Guardian

Shesha, the multi-headed serpent, plays a fundamental role in Hindu cosmology, and his association with time is profound. His name, meaning "remainder" or "that which is left over," symbolizes the enduring force that remains after the universe undergoes its periodic destruction. He is often depicted as an infinite serpent on which the god Vishnu reclines during the intervals between the cycles of creation and dissolution. Shesha is thus not only a supporter of the world, but also the bearer of the universe's time cycles, holding the cosmos together in an unbroken chain of renewal.

Each Yuga is said to correspond with different positions and movements of Shesha, who holds the world steady as it passes through each age. The cycles of Yugas are intertwined with Shesha's cosmic duties—just as he is timeless and eternal, so too are the Yugas, continuously revolving, never ceasing in their relentless progression.

Satya Yuga: The Golden Age of Truth

The Satya Yuga, also known as the Krita Yuga, is the first and most glorious of the four ages. It is described as a time when the world is bathed in divine light and purity, and all beings live in harmony with nature and the divine. This age is called the "age of truth" because truth (satya) and righteousness (dharma) prevail above all. Human beings are spiritually advanced, free from greed, suffering, and ignorance. In this epoch, there is no need for organized religion or complex rituals because every individual naturally follows dharma. It is a time of ultimate perfection where gods and men dwell together in mutual understanding.

Shesha's influence during Satya Yuga is strongest, as he represents the perfect balance of cosmic order. The serpent coils beneath Vishnu, embodying the harmonious flow of time and the sustained equilibrium of the universe.

Treta Yuga: The Age of Decline

In Treta Yuga, the balance begins to shift as dharma loses one of its legs. It is still a time of divine intervention, with avatars like Rama walking the earth to uphold righteousness, but humanity begins to deviate from the spiritual purity that marked the Satya Yuga. The moral decline that starts in Treta Yuga is the first sign of cosmic imbalance, although the world remains largely harmonious. The principles of dharma still guide human actions, though not as flawlessly as in the previous age.

Treta Yuga reflects Shesha's continued vigilance over the world, though the balance becomes more precarious. Shesha's role in maintaining order becomes more challenging, symbolizing the increasing difficulty in sustaining cosmic harmony as the ages progress.

Dvapara Yuga: The Era of Confusion

Dvapara Yuga marks a further decline, where virtue and vice are equally balanced. Dharma stands on two legs, indicating that righteousness is only partially upheld. It is a time of great conflicts, as seen in the epic battle of Kurukshetra in the Mahabharata. The spiritual power of humanity weakens considerably, and material desires and greed begin to take root in the hearts of people.

During this Yuga, Shesha's task of maintaining balance becomes more tenuous. The serpent is still coiled beneath the cosmos, but the weight of moral corruption begins to test his strength. Shesha's role is crucial in preventing total collapse, though the cycles of time continue to march inexorably toward the Kali Yuga.

Kali Yuga: The Dark Age of Chaos

The present age, Kali Yuga, is one of darkness, ignorance, and widespread moral degradation. Dharma stands on only one leg, signifying that truth and righteousness are barely upheld. This is the age of intense suffering, where materialism, selfishness, and violence overshadow spiritual growth. Humanity, in its most degenerate state, has largely forgotten its connection to the divine, and the world teeters on the edge of chaos.

Shesha's burden is greatest in this Yuga, as the cosmic order is under constant threat. The serpent's endurance symbolizes the resilience of the universe, even in its darkest hour. Despite the moral decay, Shesha holds steady, knowing that the end of the cycle is near and that dissolution will soon give way to renewal.

The Cycle of Renewal: Pralaya and Rebirth

At the end of Kali Yuga, the universe undergoes *pralaya*, a great dissolution, where all creation is destroyed and returns to a state of formlessness. But this is not the end—it is merely a pause before the cosmos is reborn. Shesha plays a crucial role in this transition, representing the continuity of time even through destruction. As Vishnu rests upon Shesha during this period of dissolution, the cosmic serpent holds within him the seeds of the next creation.

When the new cycle begins, Shesha's presence reminds us that time, like the serpent itself, is endless, coiling back upon itself in an infinite loop. The universe will once again be renewed, and the Yugas will continue their eternal dance, rising and falling in an unbroken cycle, sustained by the cosmic force of Shesha.

In this grand vision of time, the Yugas are not merely epochs of history but profound symbols of the moral and spiritual rhythms of the universe. They teach us that time is not a linear progression toward an ultimate end, but a continuous, recurring cycle of growth, decay, death, and rebirth. Just as Shesha holds the cosmos in an eternal embrace, the Yugas remind us that the forces of creation and destruction are inextricably linked, bound together in the infinite dance of time.

- Shesha and the Kalpa

In Hindu cosmology, time is measured in vast epochs known as *Kalpas*, and like the Yugas, these Kalpas are deeply intertwined with the cosmic serpent Shesha, who plays a central role in maintaining the balance and continuity of the universe. A Kalpa, often referred to as a "day of Brahma," represents an enormous span of time that comprises a complete cycle of creation, preservation, and dissolution of the universe. At the heart of this cosmic order is Shesha, the timeless and eternal serpent who supports the weight of creation and serves as a symbol of the universe's cyclical nature. As a guardian of time, Shesha's existence transcends even the Kalpas, embodying the continuity of life, death, and rebirth that defines the cosmos.

A Kalpa is not merely a measurement of time; it is a living, breathing period during which entire worlds come into existence, flourish, and eventually return to the primordial state of dissolution. Each Kalpa is composed of multiple Yugas, or ages, and once a Kalpa concludes, the universe undergoes a temporary dissolution called *pralaya* before the next Kalpa begins. Shesha is a constant presence throughout this process, underscoring the idea that even though the universe may collapse and renew itself, the fundamental forces that support its structure, such as Shesha, remain intact and eternal.

The Nature of a Kalpa

A Kalpa, which lasts for 4.32 billion human years, represents a complete cycle in the life of the cosmos. Each Kalpa is equivalent to a single day in the life of the creator god Brahma, and is followed by a night of equal length. During the day, the universe is in a state of creation and activity, while during the night, it dissolves into a state of cosmic sleep. The Kalpa is divided into 14 *Manvantaras*, each ruled by a different Manu, the progenitor of humanity. Each Manvantara lasts for 306.72 million years, and during each of these periods, creation undergoes subtle shifts, with new species, civilizations, and gods emerging.

At the end of a Kalpa, the universe enters *Maha Pralaya*, the great dissolution, where all existence dissolves back into the primordial waters, and all matter and time are absorbed into the infinite. This cycle of creation and dissolution is what defines the rhythm of cosmic existence, and Shesha, as the eternal serpent, is deeply involved in both the preservation of the cosmos during each Kalpa and the transition that occurs at the end of each cycle.

Shesha's Role in the Kalpa

Shesha, also known as Ananta Shesha (the endless Shesha), is the eternal and infinite serpent on whom Lord Vishnu, the preserver of the universe, reclines. The symbolism of this imagery is profound: Vishnu represents the divine force that sustains the universe, while Shesha represents the endless nature of time and space. Together, they signify the universe's constant state of motion, preservation, and regeneration.

In each Kalpa, as Vishnu lies on the coils of Shesha, the serpent supports the universe itself. Shesha's body, often depicted with an infinite number of heads, holds the weight of the cosmos, ensuring that the worlds within the universe remain in balance throughout the Kalpa. Shesha's name, which means "remainder" or "that which is left over," signifies his role as the enduring force that remains even after the destruction of the universe. He is a constant presence, holding together the fabric of the cosmos even when the world collapses into dissolution at the end of each Kalpa.

Shesha's relationship with the Kalpa is one of sustenance and preservation. Throughout the creation cycle, he ensures that the universe remains steady, maintaining the delicate balance of cosmic forces. He is both the anchor and the foundation upon which the universe rests, embodying stability and resilience in the face of the vast, shifting forces of creation and destruction.

The Kalpa and Cosmic Dissolution

At the end of each Kalpa, the universe undergoes *Maha Pralaya*, where everything that exists—worlds, gods, and all sentient beings—dissolves into the formless, undifferentiated state from which it arose. During this time, Shesha plays a pivotal role in holding the remnants of the universe, much like he holds the universe during creation. As the cosmic serpent, Shesha represents the eternal substratum that continues to exist even when the manifest universe ceases to be.

Shesha's presence during this time signifies the fact that while the universe may be destroyed, time itself never ends. The concept of *pralaya* does not imply a final end, but rather a pause or reset in the cosmic order. As the universe dissolves, Shesha remains coiled in the cosmic ocean, awaiting the next cycle of creation. His infinite nature reflects the endless cycles of Kalpas—each Kalpa may have a beginning and an end, but the greater cycle of time, represented by Shesha, is never-ending.

The night of Brahma, which follows the dissolution of the universe, is a time of cosmic rest. Shesha, however, is timeless, and while the universe may sleep, he continues to embody the principle of eternal time, reminding us that creation and dissolution are merely phases in a greater, unceasing process.

Shesha and Vishnu: The Eternal Union

The imagery of Vishnu reclining on Shesha is perhaps one of the most iconic in Hindu cosmology, and it holds deep philosophical significance. Vishnu, as the preserver of the universe, oversees the cosmic order, ensuring that the universe functions according to the principles of dharma. Shesha, as the serpent on whom Vishnu rests, represents the enduring foundation of time and space upon which all creation depends.

Together, they represent the dual principles of preservation and eternity. Vishnu's role is to maintain the universe within each Kalpa, while Shesha's role is to ensure that the underlying structure of the cosmos remains intact even through the cycles of dissolution and rebirth. The interaction between Vishnu and Shesha reflects the balance between change and continuity—while the manifest world undergoes constant change, the fundamental forces that support the universe, like Shesha, remain unchanged and eternal.

As each Kalpa begins, Vishnu awakens from his cosmic slumber, and creation begins anew. Shesha, ever-present, continues to support the universe as it grows and evolves. His presence ensures that time moves forward, guiding the cycles of Yugas and Manvantaras, while Vishnu ensures that the forces of creation, preservation, and destruction remain in harmony.

The Symbolism of Shesha's Infinity

Shesha is often depicted as having a nearly infinite number of heads, each of which symbolizes a different aspect of time and space. This depiction of Shesha underscores his role as the embodiment of infinity itself—just as time has no beginning or end, Shesha's heads multiply endlessly, representing the countless cycles of Kalpas that the universe will undergo.

The serpent's coiled form also holds deep symbolism. In Hindu thought, the serpent often represents the kundalini, or life force, which coils at the base of the spine and can be awakened to reach higher states of consciousness. Shesha's coils, which support the universe, similarly represent the underlying energies of creation that move in cycles, ever winding and unwinding as the universe goes through its periods of manifestation and dissolution.

The image of Shesha with his infinite coils and endless heads serves as a reminder of the vast, cyclical nature of time and the universe. Just as Shesha supports the world, his endless coils represent the infinite layers of reality and time that stretch far beyond human comprehension.

The Eternal Nature of Kalpas and the Promise of Rebirth

The concept of Kalpas and Shesha's role within them illustrates the cyclical nature of Hindu cosmology. Time, in this understanding, is not a straight line leading to an ultimate end, but an endless loop of creation, preservation, destruction, and rebirth. Shesha, as the cosmic serpent, is a reminder of the permanence of time, even in the face of impermanence.

Kalpas are not simply ages that pass and fade into oblivion. Instead, they represent the continuous unfolding of the cosmos, where each end leads to a new beginning. Shesha's presence throughout the Kalpas reassures us that even as the universe dissolves, the forces that hold it together remain, ready to bring forth new life, new worlds, and new epochs of time.

In the grand scale of cosmic time, Shesha represents the ultimate force of endurance. His unyielding nature, his support of Vishnu, and his presence through the cycles of Kalpas all speak to the Hindu belief in the eternal recurrence of all things. The universe, like the seasons, will always return to its origin, and Shesha will always be there, the steadfast guardian of time and space, ensuring the eternal flow of creation and dissolution.

Thus, Shesha and the Kalpa together symbolize the profound understanding that time, no matter how vast or cyclical, is guided by forces that are infinite, timeless, and unchanging. As the serpent coiled around the universe, Shesha serves as the enduring reminder that, in the grand dance of creation and destruction, the universe is always supported by the unbroken rhythm of time.

• The Role of Shesha in Pralaya (Cosmic Dissolution)

In the grand tapestry of Hindu cosmology, **Pralaya** refers to the period of cosmic dissolution, a time when the universe and all its elements return to their primordial state, awaiting the next cycle of creation. This dissolution occurs at the end of a Kalpa, or "day of Brahma," and is a crucial phase in the cyclical process of creation, preservation, and destruction. At the heart of this cosmic event is **Shesha**, the eternal serpent, whose role in Pralaya is both profound and symbolic. Shesha embodies the principle of eternal time, continuity, and the unbreakable link between creation and destruction, and during Pralaya, his significance is magnified, as he supports the remnants of the universe and ensures that the cosmos transitions smoothly into the next cycle.

Understanding Pralaya: The Cosmic End

Pralaya, often referred to as the "end of the world," is not to be seen as an absolute annihilation, but rather as a phase of dormancy and dissolution in the endless cycle of cosmic time. Hindu cosmology envisions time as cyclical, and the universe goes through repeated cycles of creation (*Srishti*), preservation (*Sthiti*), and dissolution (*Pralaya*). Each Kalpa, lasting 4.32 billion human years, culminates in Pralaya, where the manifested world dissolves, allowing the cosmic elements to merge back into their original, undifferentiated state.

There are different types of Pralaya, such as *Naimittika Pralaya*, which marks the end of a Kalpa, and *Mahapralaya*, the great dissolution that occurs at the end of Brahma's entire lifespan, after 100 divine years. During both these phases of cosmic dissolution, the universe, including the gods, the elements, and all forms of life, return to their primordial origins. However, time does not end; it continues in an unmanifest form, and the seeds of creation remain latent, awaiting the next cycle of emergence.

Shesha's Role in the Dissolution of the Universe

At the end of each Kalpa, the universe dissolves into the primordial waters, and everything that has been created returns to a state of non-being. During this time, Shesha plays a central role, not only as the preserver of cosmic balance but also as the very embodiment of time that continues to exist beyond creation and destruction. As the serpent of infinity, Shesha represents the substratum upon which the entire universe rests, and during Pralaya, he continues to hold the universe together, ensuring that the process of dissolution is not one of chaos but of orderly transition.

1. The Symbol of Continuity Amidst Destruction

Shesha, often depicted with his infinite coils and countless heads, is the personification of endless time. As the universe collapses into itself during Pralaya, Shesha remains an unbroken link between the end of one cycle and the beginning of the next. His presence signifies that even though the manifested universe dissolves, the fundamental principles of time, space, and cosmic order do not vanish. Rather, they exist in a latent state, preserved within the timeless coils of Shesha, waiting to manifest again in the next cycle of creation.

Shesha's symbolism as the eternal serpent reflects the Hindu understanding that destruction is not final. The process of Pralaya is part of the natural order of the universe, and Shesha's presence during this phase represents the promise of rebirth and regeneration. He is the custodian of time itself, ensuring that the cosmic cycle can continue uninterrupted.

2. Supporting Vishnu and the Seed of Creation

In Hindu mythology, Shesha is often depicted as the bed on which **Lord Vishnu**, the preserver of the universe, reclines during Pralaya. This image holds deep significance, as Vishnu's cosmic slumber on the coils of Shesha represents the dormancy of the universe during dissolution. Vishnu is the divine force that preserves the cosmos, and during Pralaya, as the universe dissolves into the primordial waters, he enters a state of deep meditation. Shesha, supporting Vishnu, represents the underlying forces of time and space that remain intact even as the universe dissolves into nothingness.

The imagery of Vishnu lying on Shesha amidst the cosmic ocean (*Ksheer Sagar*) during Pralaya signifies that the seeds of creation still exist, even within the waters of dissolution. Vishnu's sleep is not one of inactivity but rather one of potential energy. Shesha's coils, which hold Vishnu, symbolize the infinite potential of the cosmos, coiled and waiting for the moment when creation will begin anew. In this sense, Shesha represents the continuity of the cosmic order through time, even in periods of dissolution.

3. The Infinite Coils: Holding the Universe Together

Shesha's infinite form is crucial to understanding his role during Pralaya. As the cosmic serpent, he holds the universe in his countless coils, symbolizing his ability to contain and maintain the cosmos even in its most unmanifest state. During Pralaya, when all matter dissolves into the primordial waters, it is Shesha who keeps the fundamental forces of creation intact. His endless form represents the idea that time and space are never truly destroyed; they are merely uncoiled and recoiled in different forms.

Shesha's coils also represent the infinite layers of reality that continue to exist, even when the physical world dissolves. Just as Shesha has countless heads and coils, so too does the universe have countless dimensions and levels of existence, many of which remain hidden during Pralaya. His ability to support the universe in his coils signifies that the fundamental structure of reality is preserved, even in dissolution.

4. Pralaya and the Dormant Universe: Shesha as the Guardian of Time

During Pralaya, time itself appears to enter a state of dormancy. The cycles of Yugas and Kalpas come to a temporary halt, as the universe enters a phase of dissolution. However, time, as represented by Shesha, does not cease to exist. Shesha's role as the guardian of time ensures that the cosmic clock continues to tick, even though the universe may no longer be manifest. His very name, Shesha, meaning "remainder" or "that which is left over," emphasizes his role as the eternal force that remains after everything else has dissolved.

In this sense, Shesha's role during Pralaya is one of preservation—not of physical objects or beings, but of the deeper forces of time and space that underpin all existence. He ensures that time does not end, but rather transitions smoothly from one cycle of creation to the next. Shesha is both the guardian of the past and the bridge to the future, holding within him the memories of the previous Kalpas and the potential for the new ones to come.

The Promise of Renewal: Shesha and the Rebirth of the Universe

While Pralaya marks the end of a Kalpa, it is not an end in the absolute sense. It is part of the continuous cycle of the universe, which is always in a state of becoming. Shesha's role in this process is to ensure that the universe can be reborn after dissolution. He is not only the serpent of time but also the custodian of cosmic order. His presence during Pralaya guarantees that the dissolution is orderly and purposeful, not chaotic or destructive.

When the time for creation arrives again, Vishnu awakens from his cosmic sleep, and Shesha uncoils, allowing the universe to expand once more. This moment marks the transition from Pralaya back into the state of *Srishti*, or creation, and Shesha's uncoiling symbolizes the unfolding of time, space, and matter. The universe is reborn, but Shesha, ever-present, continues to hold it together, guiding it through the cycles of Yugas and Kalpas, just as he has done throughout eternity.

In this way, Shesha's role in Pralaya is not limited to dissolution but extends to the entire cycle of cosmic regeneration. He is the force that remains constant through the flux of creation and destruction, ensuring that the universe can always begin again.

The Deeper Symbolism of Shesha in Pralaya

The image of Shesha during Pralaya also carries a profound philosophical message about the nature of existence itself. In Hindu thought, the material world is seen as transient, always subject to change, decay, and dissolution. However, underlying this impermanence is the eternal, unchanging reality, represented by Shesha. His endless coils, which support the universe during its dissolution, symbolize the eternal truths and principles that remain constant even as the physical world comes and goes.

Shesha's role in Pralaya thus reflects the idea that while the world may appear to be destroyed, the deeper reality of existence is never truly lost. The universe, like time, is cyclical, and Pralaya is simply one phase in this ongoing process. Shesha embodies the eternal aspect of this cycle, the force that ensures that life, time, and space will continue, no matter how many times the universe dissolves and is reborn.

In conclusion, Shesha plays an essential role during Pralaya, not only as the force that holds the universe together during its dissolution but also as the eternal symbol of time, continuity, and cosmic order. His presence ensures that the process of dissolution is one of transformation, not destruction, and that the universe will always rise again from the depths of the cosmic ocean, ready to begin a new cycle of existence. Shesha's infinite nature reminds us that in the grand scale of cosmic time, nothing is ever truly lost—everything is part of the eternal dance of creation, preservation, and dissolution.

Chapter 5: Shesha and the Avataras of Vishnu

- **Shesha and Narayana**

In the grand mythology of Hinduism, the connection between **Shesha** and **Narayana** (another name for **Lord Vishnu**) is a symbol of eternal time, cosmic order, and divine sovereignty. Shesha, the multi-headed serpent, and Narayana, the preserver of the universe, share a relationship that is as ancient as creation itself. The imagery of Vishnu reclining on Shesha amidst the cosmic ocean of milk, known as *Ksheer Sagar*, represents the balance between time, space, and divinity, as well as the harmonious relationship between the unmanifest and manifest aspects of the cosmos.

Shesha and Narayana are depicted as being inextricably linked, with the serpent eternally serving as the bed on which Vishnu rests in his cosmic form. This profound relationship embodies the essence of creation and dissolution, as Vishnu, the preserver of the universe, is both supported and protected by Shesha, the embodiment of endless time. Their connection is one of complementary energies: while Vishnu sustains the universe and maintains the balance between good and evil, Shesha ensures that the underlying principles of time and cosmic law remain intact.

Narayana: The Cosmic Preserver

Narayana, a name that means "the one who rests on the waters" or "the refuge of all beings," is one of the most revered forms of Vishnu. He is the supreme force responsible for the maintenance of the universe, and his role as the preserver is critical in Hindu cosmology. Narayana is often depicted as reclining on the primordial waters, the endless ocean that stretches into infinity, with Shesha, the serpent of time, coiled beneath him. This cosmic image is rich in symbolism, as it represents Narayana's control over the forces of creation, preservation, and destruction.

In his cosmic form, Narayana lies in a state of deep meditation, his eyes half-closed, representing the idea that the universe exists in a state of constant balance. The universe, in this vision, is not in a state of static perfection but is constantly in motion, evolving, decaying, and being reborn in cycles. Narayana, as Vishnu, is the force that ensures these cycles run smoothly. He ensures that cosmic order is maintained, that dharma (righteousness) is upheld, and that whenever the balance of the universe is threatened, he takes form to restore order.

The name Narayana also refers to Vishnu's role as the resting place or the refuge for all beings. In this sense, the primordial waters represent the undifferentiated state from which the universe emerges and into which it dissolves at the end of each cycle. Narayana's reclining posture symbolizes the idea that even though the universe is dynamic and constantly changing, there is a deeper, unchanging reality that sustains all creation. This reality is symbolized by Shesha, who supports Narayana and the universe itself with his endless coils.

Shesha: The Support of Narayana

Shesha, also known as **Ananta**, meaning "endless" or "infinite," is depicted as a multi-headed serpent, often shown with a thousand hoods. His name itself is suggestive of his role in the cosmic order—he represents the eternal and unending nature of time, the force that underpins all creation. Shesha's primary role is to support the entire cosmos, ensuring that the cycles of creation, preservation, and destruction occur according to the divine plan. In this capacity, he serves as the bed on which Narayana reclines, symbolizing the stability and continuity of the universe.

The image of Vishnu reclining on Shesha carries multiple layers of symbolism. Shesha's coiled form represents the cyclical nature of time—just as a snake coils and uncoils, so too does time move in cycles. Shesha's endless coils suggest that time is eternal, without beginning or end, and that it is the force that sustains all of creation. Vishnu, as the preserver of the universe, is supported by Shesha's coils, which represent the flow of time and the cosmic order that ensures the universe remains in balance.

In Hindu mythology, Shesha is also seen as the foundation of the physical universe. His coils are said to hold up the earth and all the heavenly bodies, preventing them from falling into chaos. This imagery suggests that time, as represented by Shesha, is the framework upon which all of existence rests. Without time, there would be no change, no growth, no decay, and ultimately no creation or dissolution. Shesha's role as the supporter of Narayana reflects his deeper role as the sustainer of the entire cosmic process.

The Cosmic Ocean: The Waters of Creation

The imagery of Narayana reclining on Shesha is set within the **Ksheer Sagar**, the cosmic ocean of milk, which is said to be the primordial waters from which all creation arises. These waters represent the undifferentiated potential of the universe, the raw, unmanifest energy from which all things emerge and into which they return. The cosmic ocean is a symbol of the divine essence that permeates all existence, the source of life and the reservoir of all potential.

Shesha and Narayana together represent the process by which the universe is maintained and preserved within these waters. While Shesha's coils symbolize the continuity of time, Narayana's presence on the ocean represents the divine will that brings order out of chaos. The ocean itself, being endless and boundless, reflects the infinite nature of the cosmos, where time and space exist without limit.

This image of the cosmic ocean also suggests the idea of creation as a continuous process. Just as Vishnu reclines on the ocean, resting but ever-watchful, so too does the universe constantly evolve, changing from one state to another without ever truly ceasing to exist. Even during periods of cosmic dissolution (*Pralaya*), when the universe dissolves back into the primordial waters, Narayana remains, supported by Shesha, ensuring that the next cycle of creation will begin anew.

Shesha and Narayana in the Cycle of Creation

The relationship between Shesha and Narayana is central to the cyclical nature of Hindu cosmology. As time progresses through the four Yugas—Satya Yuga, Treta Yuga, Dvapara Yuga, and Kali Yuga—the universe experiences periods of purity and decline. At the end of each Kalpa, when the universe is set to dissolve in Pralaya, Narayana reclines on Shesha, waiting for the right moment to begin the process of creation again.

Shesha's role during this time is one of preservation. As the embodiment of eternal time, he ensures that even though the universe may dissolve, the underlying principles of cosmic law and order remain intact. Narayana's role is to maintain balance and ensure that the cycle of creation continues. Together, Shesha and Narayana represent the forces of time and divinity that work in harmony to sustain the universe.

In moments of cosmic dissolution, Shesha's infinite coils are said to hold the essence of the universe, ensuring that the seeds of creation are preserved. Narayana, in his role as the preserver, enters a state of deep meditation, allowing the universe to dissolve into the cosmic ocean. However, as the next cycle of creation approaches, Shesha uncoils, allowing the universe to expand once more, while Narayana awakens from his meditation and sets the process of creation into motion again.

The Spiritual Significance of Shesha and Narayana

On a deeper level, the relationship between Shesha and Narayana carries profound spiritual significance. In Hindu thought, the universe is seen as a manifestation of the divine, and the process of creation, preservation, and dissolution is an expression of the divine will. Narayana, as Vishnu, represents the divine consciousness that sustains the universe, while Shesha represents the flow of time and the cosmic order that makes creation possible.

For the devotee, the image of Narayana reclining on Shesha serves as a reminder of the eternal nature of the soul and the impermanence of the material world. Just as the universe goes through cycles of creation and dissolution, so too does the individual soul undergo cycles of birth and death. However, just as Narayana remains eternal and unchanging amidst the changing universe, so too does the soul remain untouched by the cycles of birth and death. The relationship between Shesha and Narayana symbolizes the eternal truth that underlies the transient nature of existence.

In this sense, Shesha and Narayana are not merely cosmic forces but also represent the deeper spiritual truths that govern the universe. Shesha, with his infinite coils, reminds us that time is both cyclical and eternal, and that every end is also a new beginning. Narayana, as the preserver of the universe, assures us that the divine will always maintain balance, even in times of chaos and destruction.

Shesha and Narayana in the Avataras

The relationship between Shesha and Narayana extends beyond the cosmic realm and into the incarnations of Vishnu. In several of Vishnu's avataras, Shesha accompanies him, either as his companion or as a protector. For example, in the **Rama** avatara, Shesha incarnates as **Lakshmana**, Rama's devoted brother, while in the **Krishna** avatara, Shesha takes the form of **Balarama**, Krishna's elder brother. In both cases, Shesha's role is to support and protect Vishnu in his earthly form, just as he supports him in his cosmic form.

In these avataras, Shesha's role is to ensure that Vishnu's divine mission is carried out successfully. Whether through direct protection or unwavering support, Shesha's presence highlights the unbreakable bond between time, cosmic law, and the divine will. This connection between Shesha and Narayana in their earthly forms reinforces the idea that time and divinity are inseparable, both in the cosmic realm and in the material world.

Conclusion: The Eternal Harmony of Shesha and Narayana

The relationship between Shesha and Narayana is one of the most profound symbols in Hindu mythology. It speaks to the eternal nature of the universe, the unending flow of time, and the divine order that sustains all creation. Together, they represent the balance between change and permanence, the dynamic cycles of the universe, and the unchanging reality that underlies all existence.

In the grand cosmic drama, Shesha and Narayana serve as reminders of the eternal truths that govern both the universe and the soul. While the universe may rise and fall, time may coil and uncoil, and life may go through endless cycles, the divine presence of Narayana, supported by the eternal flow of Shesha, remains ever-watchful, ensuring that the balance of the cosmos is maintained, and that life continues in its eternal dance.

- ## Shesha in the Ramayana

In Hindu mythology, **Shesha**, the multi-headed serpent and symbol of cosmic time, plays a significant yet often subtle role in the epic of the **Ramayana**. The Ramayana, composed by the sage Valmiki, narrates the story of **Lord Rama**, an incarnation of **Vishnu**, and his journey to uphold dharma (righteousness) against the forces of adharma (unrighteousness). Within this grand narrative, Shesha incarnates as **Lakshmana**, Lord Rama's devoted younger brother, emphasizing the deep cosmic relationship between Shesha and Vishnu across both divine and mortal realms.

Shesha's role in the Ramayana as Lakshmana highlights the eternal bond between time (Shesha) and preservation (Vishnu), and it reveals the serpent's unwavering dedication to supporting the divine mission of Vishnu in whatever form the preserver god takes. Lakshmana's character embodies Shesha's qualities of loyalty, selflessness, and an unshakable commitment to cosmic balance. To understand Shesha's role in the Ramayana, we must explore his incarnation as Lakshmana, the significance of his actions, and how his presence reflects deeper metaphysical themes within the epic.

Shesha as Lakshmana: The Eternal Companion

Shesha's incarnation as **Lakshmana** in the Ramayana is one of the most striking instances where the serpent deity takes a physical form to assist Vishnu in his divine mission. Lakshmana is not just Rama's brother, but his constant companion, a role mirroring Shesha's eternal presence as the bed upon which Vishnu reclines in the cosmic ocean. In the divine context, Shesha is always with Vishnu, supporting him through time and space; similarly, as Lakshmana, he accompanies Rama through the trials and tribulations of his life on earth.

Lakshmana's devotion to Rama is unparalleled. From the moment of Rama's exile to the forests to his final victory over Ravana, Lakshmana remains by his side, offering unwavering support. He abandons his own comfort, his own desires, and even his family life to serve Rama, just as Shesha sacrifices himself in the cosmic realm to uphold Vishnu's mission of preserving the universe. The relationship between Rama and Lakshmana in the Ramayana is a reflection of the eternal cosmic relationship between Vishnu and Shesha, one that transcends the boundaries of time and incarnation.

Lakshmana's sacrifice is seen most poignantly when Rama is exiled to the forest for fourteen years, following the wishes of their father, King Dasharatha. While Rama is bound by duty to obey his father's command, Lakshmana chooses to accompany him out of pure devotion. This choice is not based on any personal obligation but on a deeper cosmic connection. Just as Shesha is bound to Vishnu, Lakshmana is bound to Rama by an eternal loyalty, one that transcends familial ties. He sees his purpose as inseparable from Rama's mission and dedicates himself completely to ensuring Rama's safety and success.

Lakshmana's Devotion: A Reflection of Shesha's Selflessness

Lakshmana's selflessness and commitment to Rama's cause in the Ramayana are direct reflections of Shesha's nature in Hindu mythology. Shesha, known as the **Ananta** (the endless), is the embodiment of endless time and patience. He serves as a cosmic bed for Vishnu, but more than that, he supports the very fabric of the universe with his unyielding dedication. In the Ramayana, Lakshmana displays these same qualities, constantly sacrificing his own needs and desires for the sake of Rama.

Throughout the fourteen years of exile, Lakshmana renounces all personal comfort. He does not sleep, eat, or rest until Rama has done so. His life revolves around serving Rama and protecting him from the dangers of the forest. Just as Shesha is said to support the weight of the entire universe with his coils, Lakshmana bears the emotional and physical burdens of the exile. His actions highlight the theme of self-sacrifice, which is central to Shesha's role in the cosmic order.

One of the most striking examples of Lakshmana's selflessness comes during the construction of the **Panchavati** hermitage in the forest. While Rama and Sita rest, Lakshmana works tirelessly to build their humble abode, refusing to rest until his brother and sister-in-law are comfortable. This scene is symbolic of Shesha's role in the universe, where he tirelessly supports Vishnu's cosmic task without seeking recognition or reward. Lakshmana's humility and devotion are not just expressions of brotherly love but manifestations of the eternal bond between Shesha and Vishnu, one that transcends time and incarnation.

Lakshmana's Role in the War Against Ravana

As the Ramayana unfolds, Lakshmana's role as Rama's protector and companion becomes even more significant during the war against the demon king **Ravana**. Lakshmana's presence on the battlefield symbolizes Shesha's protective nature, as he stands by Rama's side, defending him against the forces of darkness. Just as Shesha is depicted as guarding Vishnu in his cosmic form, Lakshmana acts as Rama's shield, confronting formidable opponents with courage and skill.

Lakshmana's valor is most evident in his fierce battle with **Indrajit**, Ravana's son, who is known for his mastery of illusionary warfare. In this pivotal encounter, Lakshmana defeats Indrajit, dealing a severe blow to Ravana's forces and securing a critical victory for Rama. This moment highlights the deep bond between Rama and Lakshmana, where Lakshmana's strength and dedication prove indispensable in fulfilling Rama's divine mission. It is a reflection of how Shesha, in his cosmic form, ensures that Vishnu's divine tasks are accomplished, no matter how difficult or dangerous the obstacles may be.

However, Lakshmana's devotion is not without sacrifice. In a later battle, Indrajit manages to strike Lakshmana with a powerful weapon, leaving him gravely wounded and on the brink of death. This episode is a critical moment in the Ramayana, as it not only tests Rama's resolve but also reflects the trials faced by Shesha in his eternal service to Vishnu. Just as Shesha supports the universe through cycles of creation and destruction, Lakshmana bears the weight of suffering in his service to Rama. His near-death experience is a reminder that even divine beings must endure suffering in the mortal realm, a theme central to the Ramayana's exploration of duty, sacrifice, and devotion.

The Resurrection of Lakshmana: A Metaphor for Cosmic Renewal

The moment of Lakshmana's wounding and subsequent resurrection is one of the most symbolic episodes in the Ramayana. After being struck down by Indrajit, Lakshmana lies unconscious on the battlefield, seemingly beyond saving. It is at this point that **Hanuman**, the devoted servant of Rama, embarks on a perilous journey to retrieve the **Sanjeevani** herb from the **Dronagiri** mountain to restore Lakshmana to life. This moment of resurrection is deeply symbolic of the cyclical nature of time and existence, themes that are closely tied to Shesha's cosmic role.

In the grand cosmology of Hinduism, the universe goes through cycles of creation, preservation, and destruction. Shesha, as the embodiment of time, ensures that these cycles continue unimpeded. Lakshmana's near-death and miraculous revival mirror this cosmic process, where destruction is followed by renewal. Just as Shesha coils and uncoils in accordance with the rhythms of time, Lakshmana's resurrection symbolizes the renewal of life and the triumph of dharma over adharma.

Furthermore, Lakshmana's revival reflects Shesha's role in the preservation of cosmic balance. In Hindu mythology, Vishnu, as the preserver, relies on Shesha to maintain the equilibrium of the universe. Similarly, Rama, as an incarnation of Vishnu, depends on Lakshmana's support to fulfill his mission. Lakshmana's resurrection ensures that Rama's divine purpose can continue, just as Shesha's presence ensures that the cosmic cycles of creation and preservation remain in harmony.

Lakshmana's Role in Sita's Abandonment: The Weight of Duty

One of the more complex and emotionally charged episodes in the Ramayana is the abandonment of **Sita**, Rama's wife, after her return from captivity in Lanka. Although she has proven her chastity through the trial by fire (*Agni Pariksha*), societal doubts about her purity lead Rama to make the heart-wrenching decision to send her away to the forest. Lakshmana, ever the obedient and devoted brother, is tasked with the painful duty of escorting Sita into exile.

This episode reflects Lakshmana's unwavering adherence to duty, even when it conflicts with his personal feelings. As Shesha, Lakshmana is bound by the cosmic laws of time and duty, and his actions, no matter how painful, are in service to the greater good of maintaining cosmic balance. Lakshmana's loyalty to Rama is so profound that he suppresses his own emotional turmoil to fulfill his brother's command. In this sense, Lakshmana's role in Sita's abandonment mirrors the sacrificial nature of Shesha, who carries the weight of the universe without question or complaint.

Conclusion: Shesha's Presence in the Ramayana

Shesha's incarnation as Lakshmana in the Ramayana is a profound reflection of the eternal bond between time and divine order. Through Lakshmana's actions, we witness the selflessness, loyalty, and cosmic responsibility that define Shesha's role in the universe. Lakshmana's unwavering devotion to Rama is a manifestation of Shesha's timeless support for Vishnu, and his sacrifices on the earthly plane mirror the cosmic sacrifices that Shesha makes to maintain the equilibrium of creation.

Lakshmana's journey in the Ramayana, from his unwavering companionship to his battles on the battlefield and his emotional trials, is not just the story of a brother's love, but a deeper narrative of cosmic balance, duty, and the eternal dance between time and divinity. Through Lakshmana, the presence of Shesha in the Ramayana serves as a reminder that the forces of time and cosmic order are always at work, ensuring that dharma prevails, even in the face of immense suffering and sacrifice.

- Shesha in the Mahabharata

The presence of **Shesha**, the eternal serpent and embodiment of cosmic time, spans across multiple dimensions of Hindu mythology, and his influence extends into the grand epic of the **Mahabharata**. While the Mahabharata is primarily a story of the **Pandavas** and **Kauravas**, it is also a tale deeply woven with divine interventions, cosmic principles, and the eternal struggle between **dharma** (righteousness) and **adharma** (unrighteousness). Within this complex narrative, Shesha takes on the earthly incarnation of

Balarama, the elder brother of **Krishna**, reflecting his eternal bond with **Vishnu** and his ongoing role in maintaining cosmic balance.

Shesha's role in the Mahabharata is multifaceted, as his incarnation as Balarama mirrors his cosmic responsibilities of supporting the universe, representing time's cyclical nature, and protecting dharma. Through Balarama's actions and presence in the Mahabharata, Shesha's essence comes to life in a mortal form, showcasing his strength, wisdom, and influence on the unfolding of events. To fully appreciate Shesha's role in the Mahabharata, we must explore his incarnation as Balarama, his interactions with Krishna, his pivotal decisions, and his place in the broader cosmic and metaphysical context of the epic.

Shesha as Balarama: The Mortal Incarnation

In the Mahabharata, **Balarama** is the incarnation of Shesha, just as **Krishna** is the incarnation of Vishnu. Together, they represent the eternal partnership between time and preservation, as Shesha and Vishnu are bound by cosmic duty to uphold the universe. While Krishna's role in the Mahabharata is central and dynamic, influencing major events and guiding the Pandavas towards victory, Balarama plays a more subtle but equally important role, embodying the stability, strength, and cyclical nature of Shesha.

Balarama is depicted as a man of immense physical strength, wisdom, and righteousness. His association with agriculture and his weapon, the **plowshare**, symbolizes the nurturing and sustaining aspects of Shesha, who supports the universe in its continuous cycles. Balarama is often seen as a stabilizing force, promoting balance and fairness, much like Shesha's cosmic role of maintaining equilibrium within the universe. His presence in the Mahabharata reminds us of the importance of order and discipline in the midst of the chaos of the Kurukshetra war.

Throughout the epic, Balarama's actions reflect the timeless nature of Shesha. He is deeply attached to the principles of **dharma**, and his commitment to fairness and justice often sets him apart from other characters in the Mahabharata. While Krishna, as an incarnation of Vishnu, is more pragmatic and willing to bend the rules for the sake of dharma's ultimate triumph, Balarama is more rigid in his adherence to the laws of righteousness, much like Shesha's steadfast support of the cosmic order.

Balarama's Role in the Mahabharata: Upholding Dharma

Balarama's role in the Mahabharata is shaped by his unwavering commitment to dharma, and this aspect of his character reflects Shesha's eternal role as the upholder of cosmic balance. Balarama, although related to both the Pandavas and Kauravas, remains impartial throughout much of the epic. His neutrality in the Kurukshetra war highlights his belief in justice and fairness, qualities that are central to Shesha's cosmic duties.

One of the most significant moments in the Mahabharata where Balarama's commitment to dharma is evident is during the infamous **gambling match** between the Pandavas and Kauravas. Although Balarama is not directly involved in the match, his disapproval of the deceit and manipulation employed by **Shakuni** and **Duryodhana** is clear. Balarama, as Shesha's incarnation, values honesty and integrity, and he is deeply disturbed by the violation of dharma that occurs during the match. His disapproval foreshadows the catastrophic consequences that follow, as the Pandavas are exiled and the seeds of the Kurukshetra war are sown.

As the war approaches, Balarama's decision to remain neutral is another reflection of his commitment to dharma. While Krishna actively supports the Pandavas and helps them strategize, Balarama chooses not to take sides, despite being the elder brother of Krishna. This decision is not born out of indifference, but out of a deep sense of fairness. Balarama recognizes the righteousness in both sides—his beloved disciple **Duryodhana**, whom he admires for his strength and skill, and the Pandavas, who are fighting for justice. His neutrality underscores Shesha's cosmic role as a force that upholds balance and does not favor one side over the other unless the principles of dharma are at stake.

The Duel Between Bhima and Duryodhana: Balarama's Anguish

One of the most pivotal moments in the Mahabharata involving Balarama is the final **duel between Bhima and Duryodhana**. This duel is a culmination of the enmity between the Pandavas and Kauravas, and it ultimately decides the outcome of the war. Balarama, as Duryodhana's teacher and admirer, watches the duel with great interest, hoping that his disciple will triumph in a fair fight. Duryodhana's mastery of the **mace** (gada), taught to him by Balarama, gives him an advantage, and Balarama is confident in his disciple's prowess.

However, the duel takes a dramatic turn when Bhima, following Krishna's advice, strikes Duryodhana on the thigh, an act considered unethical in mace fighting. This moment enrages Balarama, who sees it as a violation of dharma and fair play. He is prepared to retaliate against Bhima for this dishonorable act, but Krishna intervenes, calming Balarama and reminding him of the larger purpose of the war—to restore dharma. This episode is significant because it highlights the tension between Balarama's strict adherence to the rules of combat and Krishna's more flexible approach to upholding dharma. Balarama's anger is a reflection of Shesha's commitment to cosmic law and the proper order of things.

Ultimately, Balarama's decision to restrain his anger and accept the outcome of the duel speaks to the complex nature of dharma in the Mahabharata. While Balarama values fairness and justice, he also recognizes the necessity of Krishna's actions in the larger context of restoring balance to the world. This moment illustrates the interplay between Shesha and Vishnu—while Shesha represents the stability and continuity of cosmic law, Vishnu, in his incarnations, adapts to the changing circumstances of the universe, ensuring that dharma is upheld even when the rules must be bent.

Balarama's Departure from the Battlefield: A Reflection of Shesha's Cosmic Detachment

Balarama's detachment from the violence of the Kurukshetra war is another key aspect of his character that reflects Shesha's cosmic nature. While Krishna is deeply involved in the war's strategies and outcomes, Balarama distances himself from the bloodshed, choosing instead to go on a **pilgrimage** during the height of the conflict. This decision reflects Shesha's detachment from the transient events of the material world, even as he supports the universe through his endless coils.

Balarama's pilgrimage is a symbolic retreat from the chaos of human conflict, much like Shesha's existence beyond the mortal plane. As Shesha supports the universe from the cosmic ocean, unaffected by the events of creation and destruction, Balarama remains above the fray of war, maintaining his own sense of righteousness and detachment. This pilgrimage can be seen as a reminder of the timeless nature of Shesha, who exists beyond the cycles of time and human strife, yet is always present to ensure the balance of the cosmos.

Balarama's departure from the battlefield also serves as a commentary on the futility of violence and the impermanence of human conflict. As Shesha, the eternal serpent, embodies time and its cyclical nature, Balarama's actions remind us that all wars, no matter how great, are temporary, and the principles of dharma will eventually prevail. His pilgrimage is a journey towards spiritual renewal, a reflection of the cosmic cycles that Shesha governs, where creation, destruction, and preservation are all part of the eternal dance of the universe.

Balarama's Role in the Yadava Civil War: The Final Cycle of Destruction

Towards the end of the Mahabharata, after the Kurukshetra war has ended, the Yadava clan to which Balarama and Krishna belong becomes embroiled in a destructive internal conflict. This **Yadava civil war**, fueled by internal discord and arrogance, ultimately leads to the clan's annihilation. Balarama's role in this final cycle of destruction is significant, as it mirrors Shesha's role in the cosmic dissolution (**pralaya**), where the universe is periodically destroyed to make way for new creation.

As the Yadavas descend into chaos, Balarama, much like Shesha at the end of a cosmic cycle, withdraws from the material world. He retreats to the forest, where he sits in a meditative state, preparing for his final departure from the world. In this moment, Balarama's actions reflect the dissolution of Shesha's role at the end of a **kalpa** (cosmic cycle), where time itself recedes, and the universe is engulfed in cosmic dissolution. Balarama's meditation represents the final act of detachment, where the soul prepares to merge with the infinite, just as Shesha retreats into the cosmic ocean at the end of time.

In the final moments of Balarama's life, as he leaves the material world, he is described as taking the form of a **white serpent**—Shesha's true, eternal form. This transformation is a powerful reminder of Balarama's divine nature as the incarnation of Shesha and the cyclical nature of time and existence. Just as Shesha remains beyond the reach of destruction and creation, Balarama's return to his serpent form signifies the eternal continuity of the cosmic order, even as the Yadava clan and the world around him disintegrate.

Conclusion: Shesha's Eternal Influence in the Mahabharata

Shesha's presence in the Mahabharata, through the incarnation of Balarama, is a subtle yet profound reminder of the eternal principles that govern the universe. As the upholder of time and cosmic order, Shesha's influence permeates the epic's narrative, guiding the events of the Kurukshetra war, the rise and fall of kingdoms, and the eventual restoration of dharma. Balarama's actions, decisions, and detachment from the chaos of the world reflect Shesha's timeless nature, reminding us that, in the grand scheme of the cosmos, the cycles of time, creation, and destruction are inevitable.

Through Balarama, the Mahabharata illustrates the delicate balance between stability and change, order and chaos, that Shesha upholds. As the cosmic serpent who supports the universe on his endless coils, Shesha's role in the Mahabharata is a testament to the enduring power of time, the importance of dharma, and the eternal cycles that govern all life. Balarama's journey in the epic mirrors the greater cosmic journey of Shesha, reminding us that, even in the midst of conflict and destruction, the eternal principles of the universe remain unbroken, guiding all things towards balance and renewal.

Chapter 6: Shesha in Iconography and Temples

• Iconography of Shesha

In Hindu mythology, **Shesha**, also known as **Ananta** (the endless one), occupies a significant place not only in sacred texts but also in religious art and iconography. His form is a majestic and awe-inspiring representation of timelessness, cosmic balance, and the cyclical nature of existence. As the serpent king who supports the universe and serves as the resting place for **Vishnu**, Shesha's iconography is rich with symbolic meaning. His portrayal in temples, scriptures, and artwork conveys deep spiritual truths about creation, destruction, and the eternal rhythm of life.

The visual representation of Shesha typically showcases him as a massive, multi-hooded serpent. His serpentine form, often coiled in infinite loops, suggests the vastness of cosmic time, with no discernible beginning or end. The serpentine imagery is significant, symbolizing the concept of **Kundalini** (the dormant spiritual energy within the human body) and the primal forces of creation and dissolution that govern the universe. The rich details in the iconography of Shesha not only celebrate his divine role but also offer a deeper metaphysical understanding of the cosmos itself.

Shesha as Ananta: The Infinite Serpent

One of the most prominent aspects of Shesha's iconography is his portrayal as **Ananta**, meaning infinite or endless. In Hindu cosmology, time is cyclical, represented by the eternal cycles of **yugas** and **kalpas**, and Shesha personifies this concept. His form as an endless, coiling serpent represents the continuity of time that stretches infinitely into the past and future. The visual depiction of Shesha often includes his body coiling around itself, suggesting the idea of **time looping**—a visual metaphor for the repeating cycles of creation, preservation, and destruction that define the universe.

In temples and artworks, Shesha is often depicted with **five**, **seven**, or sometimes even **a thousand hoods**, each spreading majestically over his head. The multiple hoods symbolize several layers of cosmic reality and spiritual truth, with each hood representing different aspects of time and space. The number of hoods varies based on regional traditions and the specific form of Vishnu being depicted. For instance, in some depictions, the seven hoods correspond to the seven worlds in Hindu cosmology, while in others, they reflect the seven major chakras or energy centers within the body.

The multiple hoods also emphasize Shesha's protective nature. Just as Shesha serves as a physical and metaphysical support for Vishnu, the serpent's hoods spread out to shield the divine figure from cosmic forces, signifying the protection that Shesha offers to the universe itself. His ability to safeguard the cosmos is visually communicated through this motif, suggesting that even in times of cosmic dissolution (**pralaya**), Shesha's presence remains as a constant source of protection and balance.

Vishnu Reclining on Shesha: The Iconic Representation

One of the most famous depictions of Shesha in Hindu iconography is the image of **Vishnu reclining** upon his coiled body, a pose often referred to as **Anantasayana** or the "sleep of Vishnu on Ananta." This form is seen in temple sculptures, paintings, and other forms of religious art throughout India. In this image, Vishnu, the preserver of the universe, is shown in a serene, reclining position atop Shesha, while the serpent's hoods spread out over Vishnu's head like a royal canopy.

This image symbolizes the divine cycle of **preservation** and **rest** between the destruction and recreation of the universe. Vishnu's reclining posture signifies the **yoganidra**, or cosmic sleep, during which the universe is in a state of rest, awaiting the next cycle of creation. Shesha, on whose body Vishnu rests, represents the underlying support of the universe, the eternal force that continues to exist even during the period of cosmic dissolution. The snake's coils, in which Vishnu lies, symbolize the stability of cosmic order and the cyclical nature of time, suggesting that while Vishnu sleeps, the universe remains held in balance by Shesha's eternal form.

In many depictions, **Lakshmi**, the goddess of wealth and Vishnu's consort, is also present, sitting by Vishnu's feet as he rests on Shesha. This trio of Vishnu, Lakshmi, and Shesha is a representation of the interconnectedness of **creation**, **sustenance**, and **abundance**. Shesha's coiled form represents the eternal time, Vishnu represents the preserver of the universe, and Lakshmi represents prosperity, all of which are integral to the functioning of the cosmos.

In terms of artistic depiction, the **Anantasayana** pose is elaborately carved in temples and often painted in vibrant colors. The serpent's scales are depicted in great detail, highlighting the craftsmanship involved in these depictions. The smooth yet intricate design of Vishnu reclining on Shesha portrays a sense of divine serenity and cosmic equilibrium, where the chaos of the universe is subdued in the presence of eternal forces like Shesha.

Shesha as the Support of the Cosmos

Another significant theme in Shesha's iconography is his role as the **support of the cosmos**. In this form, Shesha is not just a companion of Vishnu, but a fundamental element in the structure of the universe. Many depictions show Shesha as literally **holding up the earth** or providing the foundation for the various planes of existence. This iconographic representation highlights his role in ensuring the stability of the cosmos, both physically and metaphysically.

In certain South Indian temples, sculptures and carvings depict Shesha as a serpent coiling beneath the earth, supporting it with his strength. These depictions show his expansive body holding up mountains, rivers, and oceans, signifying his role as the bedrock of creation. This concept stems from the belief that Shesha lies at the bottom of the cosmic ocean, where he supports the earth on his massive coils. Just as a serpent provides stability with its coiled body, Shesha is depicted as the essential support structure upon which the world rests.

Shesha's cosmic role is also visually communicated through the intricate patterns of his scales, which in some representations are shown as resembling the earth's terrain, further reinforcing the idea that he is the physical foundation upon which the world exists. His coiled form is seen not as a symbol of confinement but of strength, resilience, and the ability to contain the infinite expanses of the universe within his grasp.

The Serpent of Time and Knowledge

Another layer of symbolism in Shesha's iconography is his association with **time** and **knowledge**. In Hindu philosophy, snakes are often seen as symbols of wisdom and enlightenment, and Shesha, as the king of serpents, is the ultimate representation of these qualities. His connection to time is not only through his role as Ananta, the endless one, but also through his association with the cycles of **birth**, **death**, and **rebirth**.

In certain artistic traditions, Shesha is depicted with a **third eye** or adorned with symbols associated with higher consciousness, further emphasizing his role as a guardian of knowledge. As the repository of ancient wisdom, Shesha holds the secrets of the universe, time, and creation, and his multiple hoods suggest the multiplicity of perspectives and truths that he oversees. His presence in iconography often evokes a sense of mystery and the esoteric, pointing to the hidden, unknowable aspects of the cosmos that he guards.

In some depictions, Shesha is also shown interacting with the **Nagas**, the serpent deities that are closely associated with water, fertility, and the underworld. As their king, Shesha's iconography in these contexts often places him in a position of authority and wisdom, surrounded by lesser serpentine beings who look up to him as a guide and protector.

Shesha's Role in Temples: Guardian and Protector

The presence of Shesha in Hindu temple architecture is significant, particularly in the **Vaishnava** tradition, where Vishnu is worshipped as the supreme deity. In many temples dedicated to Vishnu, Shesha is prominently displayed in both the main sanctum and throughout the temple complex. His image is often found as part of the temple's primary deity, where Vishnu is shown reclining on Shesha, or as standalone serpent imagery, protecting the temple and its visitors.

In many temple settings, Shesha serves not only as a visual representation of cosmic balance but also as a **guardian figure**, protecting the temple and its sanctity. Sculptures of serpents—particularly those with multiple heads—are placed at the entrances of temples or near sacred water bodies, symbolizing Shesha's role as a protector of the divine space. These serpentine sculptures often evoke the fearsome yet benevolent nature of Shesha, reminding devotees of his power to maintain order while warding off evil and chaos.

Temples dedicated to Vishnu, especially those that celebrate his **avatars**, frequently incorporate elaborate depictions of Shesha in their architecture. The **Ranganathaswamy Temple** in **Srirangam**, for example, features a massive sculpture of Vishnu reclining on Shesha in the sanctum sanctorum. The intricacy of Shesha's depiction in these temples reflects his deep connection to Vishnu and his importance in the overall religious experience of the temple. His form is often surrounded by symbols of water and the ocean, reinforcing his role as the cosmic serpent who resides in the **Ksheer Sagar** (Ocean of Milk), providing a sense of continuity between the divine, the earthly, and the metaphysical realms.

Shesha's Symbolism in Modern Iconography

In more contemporary depictions, Shesha continues to be an iconic figure in both religious and artistic circles. Artists often draw upon traditional representations but add modern interpretations of Shesha's cosmic role. In popular media, Shesha is depicted with a greater emphasis on his role as a cosmic protector and as the embodiment of time. His association with Vishnu and the **avatars** of Vishnu continues to be central in many new temple constructions and artistic representations.

Shesha's iconography thus remains an essential aspect of Hindu religious art, embodying profound philosophical and cosmological truths about time, creation, and the universe. His serpentine form, coiling through eternity, continues to inspire awe and reverence, reminding devotees of the unchanging, eternal forces that guide the cycles of life and existence. Through the visual language of Shesha's iconography, the eternal dance of creation and dissolution is celebrated, making him not only a figure of myth but also an enduring symbol of the cosmic order that underpins the Hindu worldview.

• Temples Dedicated to Shesha

Although **Shesha** is primarily known as the eternal serpent who serves as the cosmic bed for **Lord Vishnu**, he is also revered independently as a deity in his own right. Shesha, also called **Ananta** or the **King of Nagas**, holds a unique place in Hindu worship. He is recognized not just as the protector of Vishnu and the guardian of cosmic balance but also as a significant figure of spiritual and mythological importance. Throughout India, various temples, particularly those dedicated to **Vaishnavism**, feature **Shesha** prominently. However, there are also shrines and sacred spaces specifically honoring Shesha, where devotees come to seek his protection, wisdom, and blessings.

These temples serve as places of worship, veneration, and pilgrimage, where Shesha's association with time, cosmic order, and protection is celebrated. Shesha's presence in temple architecture and sculpture often goes beyond mere decorative elements; it represents the deep philosophical truths he embodies, particularly the infinite and cyclical nature of the universe.

The Role of Shesha in Vaishnavite Temples

In the majority of temples dedicated to **Lord Vishnu**, Shesha plays a central role. He is often depicted as a protective figure, sheltering Vishnu as he rests on the serpent's coiled body in the **Anantasayana** (reclining) posture. In such depictions, Shesha symbolizes the eternal nature of time, as Vishnu rests between cycles of creation and dissolution. The most famous of these is the **Ranganathaswamy Temple** in **Srirangam**, Tamil Nadu, where Vishnu is worshipped in his reclining form atop Shesha.

In these temples, the image of Shesha is usually monumental, with Vishnu lying in peaceful repose on Shesha's coiled body, his head resting on his right hand while Shesha's multiple hoods spread out protectively. This form is not only an artistic depiction of Shesha but a profound symbol of the inseparable connection between time (Shesha) and preservation (Vishnu). The elaborate depiction of Shesha's hoods in these temples often includes intricate carvings and ornamentation, highlighting the craftsmanship that has gone into creating these divine figures. The hoods are not merely decorative but symbolize the **seven** or **thousand planes of existence** that Shesha supports, further emphasizing his cosmic role.

The **Padmanabhaswamy Temple** in **Thiruvananthapuram, Kerala**, is another prominent Vaishnavite shrine where Shesha is venerated. Here, Lord Vishnu is worshipped as **Padmanabha**, reclining on Ananta-Shesha. The temple is renowned for its grandeur, with Vishnu depicted in the reclining posture similar to the one in Srirangam, while Shesha's massive coils support him. The temple's sanctum sanctorum houses this iconic depiction, where devotees come not only to worship Vishnu but also to honor Shesha, the eternal cosmic serpent who upholds the universe.

In these major Vaishnavite temples, while Vishnu is the central deity, Shesha's image plays an indispensable role, and special rituals are often dedicated to him. During important festivals and temple events, offerings are made to Shesha, particularly in acknowledgment of his protective nature and his cosmic significance. These temples are often situated near sacred rivers or water bodies, which further emphasizes Shesha's connection to water and fertility in Hindu cosmology.

Temples Specifically Dedicated to Shesha

While Shesha is most commonly associated with Vishnu, there are several temples where Shesha is the primary deity of worship. These temples, though less numerous, are important pilgrimage sites, where Shesha is venerated for his role as the cosmic serpent, the protector of the universe, and the god of time. The primary objective of worship in these temples is often to seek Shesha's protection from misfortune and his blessings for longevity and prosperity.

One such temple is the **Anantnag Temple** in **Kashmir**, a region historically associated with serpent worship. The town of **Anantnag** itself derives its name from Shesha, who is also called **Ananta**. This ancient temple, situated near a sacred spring, has been a major center of worship for Shesha for centuries. The temple is dedicated to **Anantnag**, a local form of Shesha, and has been a place of pilgrimage for devotees seeking protection and relief from illness, misfortune, and even negative planetary influences, which are often believed to be mitigated through the blessings of the cosmic serpent. The temple's architecture is characteristic of Kashmir's blend of Hindu and local traditions, with intricate stone carvings depicting the coiled form of Shesha and other snake deities.

Another significant temple dedicated to Shesha is the **Adisesha Temple** in **Andhra Pradesh**, where the serpent god is worshipped as **Adisesha**, the primordial form of Shesha. Here, Shesha is honored independently, though the temple also has shrines dedicated to Vishnu. The primary worship practices focus on seeking Shesha's protection, particularly in dealing with health problems, dangers posed by water bodies, and overcoming obstacles. Rituals are performed to appease Shesha during auspicious days, particularly during **Nag Panchami**, a festival dedicated to the serpent gods, where devotees offer milk, flowers, and turmeric to the deity.

The **Seshachalam Hills** in **Tirupati**, Andhra Pradesh, are also considered sacred to Shesha, and the hills are said to represent the coiled form of the great serpent. While the famous **Venkateswara Temple** on the hill is dedicated to Lord Vishnu, the entire region is considered to be the body of Shesha. Pilgrims traveling to Tirupati honor both Vishnu and Shesha during their journey, acknowledging the serpent god's role in supporting the sacred mountain. It is believed that Shesha chose to reside on these hills, and as such, many small shrines dedicated to him can be found throughout the region.

The Influence of Shesha in Nag Temples

Shesha is also closely associated with **naga** worship, which is a widespread practice in various parts of India, particularly in **South India**, **West Bengal**, and **Assam**. Temples dedicated to **Nagas**, or serpent deities, often feature Shesha prominently. In these temples, Shesha is venerated as the king of all Nagas, and the rituals performed are closely tied to fertility, protection from snake bites, and the well-being of crops and livestock.

One of the most famous naga temples is the **Mannarassala Nagaraja Temple** in **Kerala**, which is devoted to the serpent king **Nagaraja** but also honors Shesha as the supreme ruler of all serpents. This temple is a major center of serpent worship, where thousands of devotees, especially women, come to pray for fertility and the blessings of healthy children. The temple's design incorporates serpent imagery throughout, with sculptures of coiled snakes, Shesha's multiple hoods, and other naga deities placed in the temple courtyard and sacred groves surrounding the shrine. Special offerings of milk, eggs, and turmeric are made to Shesha and the other snake deities to appease their power and seek their blessings for protection and prosperity.

The festival of **Nag Panchami** is especially significant in such temples, where elaborate rituals are performed in honor of Shesha and other snake deities. Devotees create **snake idols** from clay, place them in water bodies, and offer prayers and food items like milk and ghee to Shesha, believing that his blessings will protect them from harm and bring good fortune. In these temples, Shesha is not only a figure of myth but a powerful, protective deity who ensures the well-being of both individuals and the larger community.

Shesha in Temple Rituals and Festivals

In temples where Shesha is venerated, specific rituals and festivals are observed in his honor. One of the most important festivals is **Nag Panchami**, celebrated across India, particularly in regions with a strong tradition of snake worship. On this day, Shesha and other serpent deities are worshipped to seek their blessings for protection from snake bites, disease, and other dangers. Devotees offer milk, honey, flowers, and fruits to images or idols of Shesha, often made from stone or metal.

In some temples, **abhishekam** (ritual bathing) is performed on the idols of Shesha, particularly those representing the coiled serpent. The ritual bathing is done with milk, water, and other sacred substances, symbolizing the purifying and protective aspects of Shesha. Devotees believe that through these rituals, they can invoke the protective energy of the serpent god and gain his favor for a long and prosperous life.

In Vaishnavite temples, where Shesha is depicted alongside Vishnu, **special prayers** are offered to the duo on significant occasions, such as Vishnu's **avatar-related festivals**. These prayers often emphasize Shesha's role as the eternal protector and upholder of cosmic balance. In temples where Vishnu is shown reclining on Shesha, the festival of **Anantasayana** is celebrated with great devotion. During this festival, devotees honor Vishnu's cosmic sleep on Shesha, recognizing the serpent's role in maintaining the universe's stability during the cycles of creation and destruction.

Conclusion: Shesha as the Eternal Guardian in Temples

Temples dedicated to Shesha or featuring his iconography offer a profound understanding of his role in Hindu cosmology and religious practice. As a protector, preserver, and guardian of time, Shesha occupies a significant place in temple worship, not only as a companion to Vishnu but as a powerful deity in his own right. The temples that honor Shesha reveal the deep spiritual and symbolic importance of the eternal serpent in Hindu belief, where

4o

ChatGPT said:

ChatGPT

his cosmic significance is celebrated through intricate iconography, dedicated rituals, and vibrant festivals. Through these temples, Shesha's divine presence continues to inspire devotion and awe, reminding us of the eternal dance of creation and dissolution that governs the universe.

- The Serpent King in Modern Devotion

In the contemporary landscape of Hindu devotion, the figure of **Shesha**—often referred to as **Ananta**, the eternal serpent king—retains a significant role both as a symbolic and venerated deity. His profound influence on religious practice and cultural expressions persists in modern times, reflecting his enduring importance in the cosmology and spiritual life of millions of devotees. This exploration delves into the evolving significance of Shesha in modern devotion, encompassing how he is worshipped, perceived, and integrated into contemporary Hindu practices and beliefs.

The Enduring Symbolism of Shesha

Shesha, often depicted as a colossal serpent coiled around the universe, symbolizes eternity, infinity, and the cyclical nature of time. His role as the cosmic bed of **Lord Vishnu** links him directly to the preservation and stability of the universe. In modern devotion, Shesha's symbolism extends beyond traditional religious practices to influence various aspects of contemporary spirituality and cultural expressions.

In an era where secularism and modernization often challenge traditional practices, Shesha's representation of timelessness and stability provides a reassuring counterpoint to the rapidly changing world. He embodies the eternal truths of Hindu cosmology, offering a sense of continuity and permanence amidst the flux of modern life. This enduring symbolism makes him a figure of contemplation and reverence for those seeking to anchor themselves in spiritual traditions.

Shesha in Contemporary Worship Practices

In modern Hindu worship, Shesha's veneration continues in both traditional and innovative forms. Temples dedicated to Shesha, or featuring his iconography, play a crucial role in preserving ancient rituals while adapting to contemporary needs. These temples serve as focal points for devotees seeking his blessings, particularly in regions where serpent worship remains strong.

1. Temples and Shrines:

Modern temples that honor Shesha often integrate traditional iconography with contemporary architectural styles. For example, in urban settings where space is limited, smaller shrines dedicated to Shesha may be established within larger temples or community centers. These shrines continue to feature the classic depictions of Shesha with multiple hoods, coiled bodies, and intricate carvings, but they may also incorporate modern artistic elements that resonate with today's aesthetic sensibilities.

In these temples, traditional rituals are observed with adaptations that reflect contemporary lifestyles. Offerings and prayers to Shesha often include symbolic items such as flowers, milk, and turmeric, alongside modern practices like meditation and wellness workshops. The integration of Shesha's worship into modern temple activities highlights his relevance in addressing both spiritual and practical aspects of contemporary life.

2. Festivals and Rituals:

Modern festivals dedicated to Shesha, such as **Nag Panchami**, have evolved to include new forms of celebration that reflect current cultural trends. While traditional practices—such as the offering of milk and the creation of clay snake idols—are still prevalent, contemporary celebrations may also feature educational programs, community outreach, and cultural performances. These adaptations help to engage younger generations and urban communities, fostering a connection to traditional worship through contemporary means.

In addition to traditional festivals, new rituals and observances have emerged that incorporate Shesha's symbolism into daily life. For example, some devotees practice meditation or recite mantras dedicated to Shesha to invoke his protective and stabilizing energies. These practices often blend ancient traditions with modern mindfulness techniques, creating a dynamic form of devotion that resonates with contemporary spiritual seekers.

Shesha in Popular Culture and Media

The figure of Shesha has also found a place in popular culture and media, reflecting his continued significance in the public consciousness. In literature, art, and entertainment, Shesha is portrayed in various forms that bridge traditional mythology with modern sensibilities.

1. Literature and Art:

Modern literary works and artistic representations often explore Shesha's symbolism in creative ways. Authors may weave Shesha into contemporary novels or spiritual texts, using his character to explore themes of eternity, time, and cosmic order. Artistic depictions of Shesha, from traditional paintings to digital media, often highlight his grandeur and mystique, offering new interpretations of his role in Hindu mythology.

In visual art, Shesha is sometimes depicted in innovative styles that blend traditional iconography with contemporary aesthetics. For instance, modern sculptures or murals may represent Shesha in abstract forms, using color and design to convey his cosmic presence. These artistic expressions help to keep Shesha's mythology alive and relevant, resonating with audiences who might otherwise be disconnected from traditional religious practices.

2. Media and Entertainment:

Shesha has also appeared in various forms of media, including films, television shows, and video games, where his character is often integrated into narratives that appeal to modern audiences. In these contexts, Shesha may be portrayed as a powerful deity or a mystical being with control over time and space. Such portrayals often emphasize his protective and stabilizing qualities, making him an intriguing and relatable figure for contemporary viewers.

The inclusion of Shesha in popular media not only serves to entertain but also educates a broader audience about his significance in Hindu cosmology. By presenting Shesha in accessible and engaging formats, modern media helps to perpetuate his mythological role and cultural relevance, ensuring that his ancient symbolism continues to inspire and inform.

Shesha and Contemporary Spirituality

In the realm of contemporary spirituality, Shesha's role extends beyond traditional worship to influence various aspects of personal and communal spiritual practice. His symbolism is often invoked in meditation, yoga, and wellness practices, where his attributes of stability, protection, and timelessness resonate with those seeking inner peace and balance.

1. Meditation and Yoga:

In meditation and yoga practices, Shesha is frequently invoked as a symbol of eternal stability and cosmic support. Practitioners may meditate on Shesha's image or recite mantras dedicated to him, seeking his assistance in achieving mental and emotional equilibrium. The concept of Shesha as the cosmic serpent who supports Vishnu's divine repose aligns well with the goal of achieving a state of inner calm and spiritual repose.

Yoga practitioners, particularly those interested in the philosophical underpinnings of Hindu thought, may incorporate Shesha's symbolism into their practice to deepen their understanding of the interconnectedness of the universe. The serpent's coiled form is often used as a metaphor for the dormant spiritual energy within each individual, which can be awakened and harnessed through disciplined practice.

2. Community and Ritual Practices:

In community settings, modern devotion to Shesha often involves collective rituals and celebrations that emphasize his protective and nurturing aspects. Community gatherings, often organized around festivals like Nag Panchami, may include rituals, cultural performances, and educational programs designed to foster a sense of shared spiritual heritage. These events provide opportunities for individuals to connect with Shesha's symbolism in a communal setting, reinforcing the bonds of devotion and cultural continuity.

Additionally, contemporary spiritual practices may integrate Shesha's iconography into personal rituals and daily routines. For instance, individuals might keep images or statues of Shesha in their homes, using them as focal points for meditation, prayer, or reflection. This personal devotion helps to maintain a connection to Shesha's cosmic attributes, offering a sense of stability and support in everyday life.

Challenges and Opportunities in Modern Devotion

The integration of Shesha into modern devotion presents both challenges and opportunities. On one hand, the rapid pace of modernization and globalization can sometimes lead to a dilution of traditional practices. The challenge lies in preserving the essence of Shesha's worship while adapting it to contemporary contexts.

On the other hand, the evolving nature of modern spirituality provides opportunities to reimagine and reinterpret Shesha's role in ways that resonate with today's diverse and dynamic society. By embracing new forms of expression and engagement, contemporary devotees can keep Shesha's symbolism relevant and vibrant, ensuring that his cosmic significance continues to inspire and uplift.

Conclusion: The Eternal Serpent in Modern Times

The figure of Shesha, the eternal serpent king, occupies a unique and enduring place in modern Hindu devotion. His symbolism as the embodiment of eternity, cosmic order, and stability continues to resonate in contemporary spiritual practices, cultural expressions, and popular media. As Hinduism navigates the complexities of the modern world, Shesha remains a powerful and inspiring symbol of the eternal truths that underpin the universe.

Through temples, festivals, art, media, and personal spiritual practices, Shesha's influence extends beyond traditional boundaries, reflecting his continued relevance and significance. His role as the cosmic serpent who supports Vishnu and maintains the balance of the cosmos remains a profound reminder of the timeless and eternal forces that guide our lives and the universe itself.

Chapter 7: Shesha's Connection with the Naga Kingdom

- The Nagas in Hindu Mythology

Introduction to the Naga Kingdom

In the rich tapestry of Hindu mythology, the Nagas emerge as a distinctive and enigmatic group of serpentine beings. The term **Naga** generally refers to a class of divine or semi-divine serpents who inhabit the underworld, known as **Patala**, and possess significant spiritual and cosmological roles. These serpentine entities are not merely mythical creatures; they symbolize profound spiritual concepts and are integral to various mythological narratives and cosmological frameworks within Hindu tradition.

The Nagas are often depicted as beings with a human upper body and the lower body of a serpent, or sometimes entirely serpentine in form. This dual nature reflects their connection to both the earthly and the divine realms. Their representation varies from powerful deities to revered ancestors, demonstrating their multifaceted role in Hindu belief systems.

Origin and Genealogy of the Nagas

The origins of the Nagas are rooted in ancient Hindu texts, with references found in the **Vedas**, **Puranas**, and epics like the **Mahabharata** and the **Ramayana**. The genealogical lineage of the Nagas often intertwines with that of other divine beings, reflecting their complex place in Hindu cosmology.

1. Vedic References:

In the **Rigveda**, the Nagas are initially referred to in a somewhat ambiguous manner, often associated with serpentine deities or powers of the earth. They are described as beings with both protective and destructive attributes. Their association with water and fertility is also emphasized, suggesting an integral role in sustaining life and natural cycles.

2. Puranic Accounts:

The **Puranas** provide a more detailed account of the Nagas. According to texts like the **Bhagavata Purana** and the **Padma Purana**, the Nagas are descendants of **Kashyapa**, one of the primordial sages, and his wife **Kadru**, who was a daughter of Daksha. This lineage places the Nagas within a broader cosmological context, linking them to the creation myths and divine ancestry.

3. Epic Narratives:

In the **Mahabharata** and the **Ramayana**, the Nagas are depicted as powerful entities with significant roles in the unfolding of the epic's narratives. Their interactions with human heroes and gods illustrate their importance in the cosmic order and their impact on the earthly realm.

The Naga Kingdom: Patala

The Naga kingdom, known as **Patala**, is an underworld realm that contrasts with the celestial and earthly realms. Patala is often described as a subterranean realm, rich in precious gems and metals, and is considered both a place of wealth and a domain of serpentine beings.

1. Description and Features:

Patala is depicted as a vibrant and opulent underworld, featuring luxurious palaces and lush gardens. The realm is not merely a place of darkness and confinement but is portrayed as a significant and lush domain with its own distinct ecological and spiritual characteristics.

2. Governance and Inhabitants:

The Nagas of Patala are ruled by various powerful serpent kings, among whom **Vasuki** and **Shesha** are the most prominent. **Vasuki**, known for his role in the churning of the ocean (Samudra Manthan), is often depicted as a significant figure who lends his support to various divine activities. **Shesha**, as the eternal serpent, upholds the universe and maintains cosmic stability from his position in the cosmic ocean.

3. Interactions with Other Realms:

Patala serves as a crucial intermediary between the celestial and earthly realms. The Nagas are frequently depicted interacting with gods, sages, and heroes, reflecting their role as custodians of certain cosmic and earthly functions. This interaction underscores their importance in maintaining the balance of cosmic order.

The Role of the Nagas in Hindu Cosmology

The Nagas' role in Hindu cosmology is multifaceted, encompassing aspects of both destruction and preservation. They are associated with various natural and supernatural phenomena, and their symbolism extends to the deeper metaphysical aspects of Hindu philosophy.

1. Symbolism of the Serpent:

In Hindu symbolism, the serpent represents multiple aspects, including fertility, immortality, and renewal. The Nagas embody these qualities through their regenerative powers and their role in sustaining the cosmic order. Their presence in mythological narratives often signifies the duality of creation and destruction, reflecting the cyclical nature of existence.

2. The Churning of the Ocean:

One of the most significant roles of the Nagas is their involvement in the **Samudra Manthan** or the churning of the ocean. During this cosmic event, the Naga king Vasuki serves as the churning rope, demonstrating the Nagas' integral role in the process of cosmic creation and the extraction of divine nectar (amrita). This event highlights the Nagas' contributions to the sustenance of both divine and earthly realms.

3. Protective and Ancestral Roles:

The Nagas are also revered as protective deities and ancestral spirits. In many regions of India, particularly in the South, serpent worship is prevalent, and Nagas are considered guardians of household and agricultural prosperity. Rituals and ceremonies dedicated to the Nagas are conducted to seek protection and blessings, reflecting their continued relevance in local religious practices.

The Nagas in Rituals and Worship

The worship of Nagas involves a variety of rituals and ceremonies that reflect their importance in Hindu devotional practices. These rituals often emphasize their protective and beneficial aspects, integrating them into the broader spectrum of Hindu worship.

1. Nag Panchami:

One of the primary festivals dedicated to the Nagas is **Nag Panchami**, celebrated annually on the fifth day of the bright half of the lunar month of Shravana (July-August). This festival involves the worship of serpentine deities and is marked by offerings of milk, prayers, and rituals to seek protection from snake bites and other calamities.

2. Ritual Offerings and Temples:

Temples dedicated to Nagas often feature elaborate serpent iconography and rituals. Offerings made to the Nagas include milk, honey, and other traditional items. These temples serve as important centers for the worship and veneration of Nagas, reflecting their ongoing significance in Hindu devotional life.

3. Regional Variations:

In different regions of India, the worship of Nagas may vary. In South India, serpent worship is particularly prominent, with dedicated shrines and festivals celebrating the Nagas' role in local religious practices. These regional variations highlight the adaptability and integration of Naga worship into diverse cultural contexts.

The Nagas in Contemporary Context

In contemporary times, the worship and veneration of the Nagas continue to hold significance. Modern practices and interpretations often reflect both traditional beliefs and contemporary spiritual needs.

1. Preservation of Tradition:

Efforts are made to preserve traditional rituals and practices related to Naga worship, ensuring that ancient customs continue to be practiced and passed down through generations. This preservation maintains the cultural and spiritual continuity of Naga worship.

2. Modern Interpretations:

Contemporary interpretations of Naga symbolism often incorporate modern spiritual and ecological concerns. The reverence for Nagas as protectors of nature and maintainers of cosmic balance resonates with contemporary values related to environmental conservation and holistic living.

3. Influence on Popular Culture:

The depiction of Nagas in popular culture, including literature, art, and media, reflects their ongoing relevance and appeal. Modern portrayals often blend traditional mythology with contemporary themes, making the Naga figures accessible and engaging to a wider audience.

Conclusion

The Nagas, as serpentine deities within Hindu mythology, occupy a unique and multifaceted position within the pantheon of divine beings. Their roles as protectors, custodians of natural and cosmic order, and symbols of renewal and eternity illustrate their deep significance in Hindu cosmology. Through their interactions with gods, sages, and humans, the Nagas embody the dynamic and interconnected nature of the universe, bridging the realms of the celestial and the earthly.

The worship of the Nagas, encompassing ancient rituals and modern adaptations, continues to reflect their enduring relevance in Hindu spiritual practices. As symbols of cosmic balance and natural forces, the Nagas remain a profound and inspiring aspect of Hindu devotion, embodying timeless truths that resonate through both traditional and contemporary contexts.

- Patala and the Underworld

Introduction to Patala

In Hindu cosmology, **Patala**—the underworld or subterranean realm—holds a distinct and multifaceted position within the cosmic order. Often translated as "the netherworld" or "the underworld," Patala is one of the seven realms that lie beneath the earth's surface, according to traditional Hindu beliefs. It is a domain rich in symbolism and divine significance, serving as both a literal and metaphorical representation of the deeper, hidden aspects of the universe.

Patala is depicted as a place that contrasts sharply with the celestial realms of the gods and the earthly plane of human existence. It is often described as a realm of great beauty and opulence, despite its subterranean location. This realm is intricately connected to various aspects of Hindu cosmology, including the roles and characteristics of the Nagas, the cosmic serpent beings, and the broader structure of the universe.

The Structure and Features of Patala

1. The Physical Description:

Patala is typically portrayed as a vast and luxurious realm lying beneath the earth's surface, comprising multiple layers or levels. Each level is associated with different qualities and features, ranging from lush gardens to magnificent palaces made of precious stones. Unlike the commonly perceived notion of an underworld as a dark and grim place, Patala is depicted as a vibrant and rich environment, filled with beauty and splendor.

2. The Realm of the Nagas:

Patala is renowned as the primary residence of the **Nagas**, the serpentine deities of Hindu mythology. These beings, who are often depicted as having a human upper body and a serpent lower body, occupy this underworld realm, and their presence is integral to the characteristics of Patala. The Nagas, including prominent figures such as **Vasuki** and **Shesha**, are depicted as both protectors and rulers of this domain, and their interaction with Patala shapes the realm's nature and significance.

3. The Richness of Patala:

In the mythological narratives, Patala is described as an extraordinarily affluent realm, abundant with valuable gems, metals, and divine treasures. The wealth of Patala is often associated with its role as a source of precious materials and artifacts, which are considered essential for various cosmic functions and divine activities. This abundance highlights Patala's significance as a crucial part of the cosmic economy and its connection to the divine and material aspects of existence.

The Cosmological Role of Patala

1. The Balance of the Cosmic Realms:

Patala plays a crucial role in the broader structure of the universe, serving as one of the seven realms or lokas in Hindu cosmology. Each of these realms is part of a cosmic system that includes the celestial heavens, the earthly plane, and the netherworld. Patala's position beneath the earth highlights its role in maintaining the balance and order of the universe, ensuring that all realms function harmoniously within the cosmic structure.

2. The Connection to Cosmic Forces:

The interactions between Patala and other cosmic forces are central to Hindu cosmology. The realm is often depicted as being involved in significant cosmic events, such as the **Samudra Manthan** (churning of the ocean), where Patala's wealth and resources play a crucial role. The churning of the ocean, which involved the Nagas as the churning rope, symbolizes the extraction of divine nectar and the interaction between various cosmic entities, including those residing in Patala.

3. The Role in Creation and Dissolution:

Patala's role in the cycles of creation and dissolution is also significant. The underworld is often associated with the process of cosmic dissolution or **Pralaya**, where the universe undergoes a period of rest and renewal. During such times, Patala serves as a domain where certain cosmic activities and transformations occur, reflecting its integral role in the cyclical nature of the universe.

Patala and Its Inhabitants

1. The Nagas:

The Nagas are the most prominent inhabitants of Patala, and their characteristics and roles are closely tied to the realm. As divine serpents, the Nagas are seen as both protectors and rulers of Patala, and their presence adds to the realm's significance. The Nagas are depicted as possessing great wisdom and power, and their interactions with other divine beings and the earthly realm often influence the cosmic balance.

2. Other Denizens:

In addition to the Nagas, Patala is also home to various other beings, including powerful Asuras (demon-like beings) and other divine or semi-divine entities. These inhabitants contribute to the diverse and dynamic nature of Patala, reflecting its status as a realm of both divine and supernatural significance.

Patala in Hindu Texts and Mythology

1. Vedic References:

The concept of Patala is referenced in the Vedic texts, where it is often associated with the netherworld and its serpentine deities. While the Vedic references may not provide a detailed description of Patala, they establish the underworld as an important component of the cosmic order.

2. Puranic Accounts:

The **Puranas** offer more detailed descriptions of Patala, including its features, inhabitants, and significance. Texts such as the **Bhagavata Purana** and the **Padma Purana** provide elaborate accounts of the underworld, highlighting its opulence and its role in the cosmic narrative. These texts describe Patala as a realm of great beauty and wealth, governed by the Nagas and involved in various divine activities.

3. Epic Narratives:

In the **Mahabharata** and the **Ramayana**, Patala is depicted as a significant realm with connections to key mythological events and characters. The underworld is often portrayed as a place where important interactions and transformations occur, influencing the outcomes of epic narratives and cosmic events.

The Symbolic Significance of Patala

1. The Underworld as a Symbol:

Patala represents more than just a physical realm; it serves as a symbolic representation of the hidden and mysterious aspects of existence. The underworld is often associated with the unconscious, the unknown, and the deeper layers of reality. As such, Patala embodies the concept of exploring and understanding the unseen dimensions of life and the cosmos.

2. The Balance of Opposites:

The existence of Patala highlights the balance between different cosmic realms. Just as the celestial heavens represent the divine and the transcendent, Patala represents the hidden and the subterranean aspects of existence. This balance is essential for maintaining the harmony and stability of the universe.

3. The Role of Wealth and Resources:

Patala's association with wealth and precious resources underscores its importance in the cosmic economy. The treasures found in Patala are not merely material assets; they symbolize the underlying abundance and richness that sustain the universe and support divine functions.

Patala in Contemporary Context

1. Preservation of Tradition:

Despite the passage of time, the concept of Patala continues to be relevant in Hindu tradition and cultural practices. Rituals and worship related to the Nagas and the underworld realm are preserved and maintained through religious practices and festivals. These traditions help to keep the significance of Patala alive in contemporary contexts.

2. Modern Interpretations:

In modern interpretations, Patala is often viewed through the lens of mythology, spirituality, and cultural symbolism. Contemporary discussions about Patala may focus on its role as a metaphor for exploring deeper aspects of the self and the universe. This reinterpretation reflects the ongoing relevance of Patala in spiritual and philosophical contexts.

3. Influence on Popular Culture:

Patala's depiction in popular culture, including literature, art, and media, reflects its enduring appeal and significance. Modern portrayals often blend traditional mythological elements with contemporary themes, making the concept of Patala accessible and engaging to a broader audience.

Conclusion

Patala, as the underworld realm in Hindu cosmology, represents a complex and multifaceted aspect of the universe. Its depiction as a place of beauty and wealth, inhabited by the Nagas and other divine beings, highlights its significance in maintaining cosmic balance and order. The symbolism associated with Patala, including its role in creation, dissolution, and hidden aspects of existence, underscores its importance in Hindu mythology and spiritual thought.

As a realm that bridges the celestial and the earthly, Patala serves as a reminder of the interconnectedness of all aspects of the cosmos. Its continued relevance in contemporary spiritual practices, cultural expressions, and popular media reflects the enduring significance of this enigmatic and powerful domain. Through its rich symbolism and profound roles, Patala continues to inspire and engage those who seek to understand the deeper dimensions of existence and the cosmic order.

- Shesha as a Protector of Treasures

Introduction

In the vast expanse of Hindu mythology, **Shesha**, the primordial serpent and cosmic deity, holds a revered position as the protector of treasures. His role transcends mere guardianship, intertwining with profound cosmic functions and spiritual symbolism. Shesha, also known as **Ananta**, which means "endless" or "eternal," is not only a symbol of the infinite and the eternal but also a custodian of the divine riches and treasures that sustain the universe. This role reflects his profound influence in maintaining the cosmic balance and safeguarding the divine wealth that upholds the natural order.

The Symbolism of Shesha as Protector

1. Shesha's Symbolic Role:

Shesha embodies the concept of infinity and eternity, being the endless serpent upon which the entire cosmos rests. His endless coils symbolize the infinite nature of the universe, and his role as a protector of treasures reflects the sacredness and significance of these divine riches. By safeguarding these treasures, Shesha ensures that the cosmic order remains intact and that the divine wealth is preserved for the benefit of all realms.

2. Connection to Cosmic Stability:

In Hindu cosmology, Shesha's role as a protector of treasures is closely linked to his function in maintaining cosmic stability. As the serpent who supports the world and the divine entities, Shesha's guardianship of treasures signifies his crucial role in preserving the equilibrium of the universe. The treasures he protects are not merely material possessions but are emblematic of the divine order and cosmic harmony.

The Treasures of Shesha

1. The Wealth of the Underworld:

Shesha's domain, Patala, the underworld, is renowned for its vast and opulent wealth. The underworld is depicted as a realm rich in precious gems, metals, and divine artifacts. Shesha, as the ruler of this domain, is intrinsically connected to these treasures. His protection of Patala's wealth signifies his role in safeguarding the cosmic resources that are essential for the sustenance and functioning of the universe.

2. Divine Artifacts and Celestial Treasures:

In addition to the material wealth of Patala, Shesha also protects various divine artifacts and celestial treasures. These include items of great spiritual significance, such as the nectar of immortality (amrita) and sacred relics that hold cosmic power. Shesha's guardianship of these artifacts underscores his role in preserving the divine and sacred elements that are central to the functioning of the universe and the well-being of the gods and sages.

3. The Role in Cosmic Events:

Shesha's protection of treasures is not limited to the underworld. He plays a vital role in significant cosmic events, such as the **Samudra Manthan** (churning of the ocean). During this event, Shesha is depicted as supporting Mount Mandara, which was used as a churning rod to extract amrita from the ocean. His involvement in such cosmic activities highlights his role in ensuring that divine treasures are both preserved and utilized for the benefit of the cosmos.

Shesha's Guardianship in Hindu Texts

1. Vedic References:

In the Vedic texts, Shesha is initially referenced in a somewhat abstract manner, with less emphasis on his role as a protector of treasures. The Vedic hymns mention serpentine deities and cosmic serpents, laying the foundation for Shesha's later significance. The concept of a cosmic serpent supporting the universe is present in these early texts, establishing the basis for his role as a guardian.

2. Puranic Descriptions:

The **Puranas** provide a more detailed account of Shesha's guardianship. The **Bhagavata Purana** and the **Padma Purana** describe Shesha as the eternal serpent who upholds the world and protects the treasures of Patala. These texts elaborate on his role in various cosmic events and his connection to divine wealth, illustrating the depth of his guardianship.

3. Epic Narratives:

In the **Mahabharata** and the **Ramayana**, Shesha's role as a protector of treasures is reflected in his interactions with other deities and heroes. His involvement in the churning of the ocean, where he supports the cosmic process and helps retrieve divine nectar, underscores his significance in safeguarding and managing celestial treasures.

The Importance of Shesha's Protection

1. Preservation of Divine Wealth:

Shesha's guardianship is crucial for the preservation of divine wealth. The treasures he protects are not only valuable but also essential for maintaining cosmic order and fulfilling the needs of the gods and the universe. His role ensures that these resources are safeguarded from misuse or depletion, preserving their sanctity and significance.

2. Maintenance of Cosmic Balance:

The protection of treasures by Shesha is integral to maintaining cosmic balance. The wealth and artifacts he guards are vital for various cosmic functions, including creation, sustenance, and dissolution. By ensuring the safety and proper management of these treasures, Shesha contributes to the stability and harmony of the universe.

3. Symbolism of Eternal Guardianship:

Shesha's role as a protector of treasures symbolizes the eternal nature of divine guardianship. His endless coils and eternal existence reflect the ongoing and unwavering commitment to safeguarding the cosmic resources and ensuring their continued availability for the divine and earthly realms.

Shesha's Guardianship in Rituals and Worship

1. Ritual Offerings and Temples:

In Hindu temples and rituals, Shesha is often honored through offerings and prayers that reflect his role as a protector of treasures. Rituals dedicated to Shesha may include offerings of precious materials, symbolic of the divine wealth he guards. Temples dedicated to Shesha or the Nagas often feature elaborate serpent iconography and serve as centers for worship and veneration.

2. Festivals and Celebrations:

Festivals and celebrations related to Shesha may emphasize his role in protecting divine treasures and ensuring cosmic stability. These events often involve rituals that seek blessings from Shesha for prosperity, protection, and the preservation of sacred resources. The celebration of Shesha's guardianship reflects the continued relevance of his role in contemporary spiritual practices.

Shesha's Guardianship in Contemporary Context

1. Preservation of Tradition:

The traditional role of Shesha as a protector of treasures continues to be recognized and honored in Hindu practices and cultural traditions. The rituals, festivals, and worship associated with Shesha maintain the relevance of his guardianship and ensure the preservation of ancient customs and beliefs.

2. Modern Interpretations:

Contemporary interpretations of Shesha's role may focus on his symbolic significance as a guardian of spiritual and material resources. Modern discussions may explore how Shesha's guardianship reflects broader themes of preservation, balance, and responsibility in both spiritual and worldly contexts.

3. Influence on Popular Culture:

The depiction of Shesha in popular culture, including literature, art, and media, reflects his enduring significance and appeal. Modern portrayals often blend traditional mythology with contemporary themes, making Shesha's role as a protector of treasures accessible and engaging to a wider audience.

Conclusion

Shesha, as the protector of treasures, embodies a profound and multifaceted role within Hindu cosmology. His guardianship of the divine wealth and sacred artifacts is essential for maintaining cosmic stability and preserving the sacred resources of the universe. Through his role in significant cosmic events, his presence in ancient texts, and his continued veneration in rituals and worship, Shesha remains a central figure in the spiritual and mythological landscape.

As a symbol of eternal guardianship and cosmic balance, Shesha's role reflects the deep interconnection between the divine, the material, and the spiritual realms. His ongoing relevance in contemporary practices and cultural expressions highlights the enduring significance of his guardianship and the timeless truths embodied in his divine presence.

Chapter 8: Shesha's Place in Hindu Cosmology
- The Serpent as a Cosmic Foundation

Introduction

In Hindu cosmology, the serpent—embodied by the deity **Shesha**—occupies a fundamental and profound role as the cosmic foundation. The serpentine form of Shesha, also known as **Ananta**, is emblematic of a deep and intricate understanding of the universe, bridging the divine and the material. His role as the cosmic serpent extends beyond mere symbolism, encompassing critical functions in maintaining the balance, stability, and continuity of the cosmic order. This chapter delves deeply into the various dimensions of Shesha's role as a cosmic foundation, exploring his symbolic significance, cosmological functions, and the broader implications of his presence in Hindu thought.

The Serpent in Hindu Cosmology

1. Shesha as the Cosmic Serpent:

In Hindu mythology, Shesha is depicted as an enormous serpent with countless coils, upon which the cosmos rests. His name, **Ananta**, means "endless" or "eternal," reflecting his role in embodying the infinite nature of the universe. Shesha's vast and endless form symbolizes the boundless and continuous nature of cosmic existence. He is often portrayed coiled around the divine figures, such as Vishnu, representing his role as a cosmic support structure.

2. Symbolism of the Serpent:

The serpent, as a symbol in Hindu cosmology, represents several key concepts:

- **Eternity and Continuity:** The serpent's endless coils reflect the infinite nature of time and existence. Shesha's role in upholding the cosmos signifies the continuity and perpetuity of the universe.

- **Support and Stability:** As the cosmic foundation, Shesha provides the support necessary for the stability of the universe. His presence ensures that the cosmic realms are anchored and maintained in their proper order.

- **Transformation and Renewal:** Serpents are also associated with transformation due to their shedding of skin. This aspect of Shesha's symbolism highlights the cyclical nature of creation, preservation, and dissolution in the cosmic process.

Shesha's Cosmological Functions

1. Upholding the Universe:

Shesha's primary function in Hindu cosmology is to uphold and support the universe. His endless coils provide a stable foundation for the cosmos, ensuring that all cosmic realms, including the earth, heavens, and underworld, remain in their designated places. This role is crucial in maintaining the balance and harmony of the universe.

2. Role in Creation:

In the process of creation, Shesha plays a significant role. According to the Puranic texts, the universe is often depicted as emerging from the cosmic ocean (Kshir Sagar), with Shesha serving as a support during the churning of the ocean (Samudra Manthan). His role in these processes underscores his importance in the foundational aspects of cosmic creation and order.

3. Participation in Cosmic Events:

Shesha's involvement in major cosmic events, such as the churning of the ocean and the cosmic dissolution (Pralaya), illustrates his integral role in the cyclical processes of the universe. His support during these events ensures that the divine activities and transformations occur smoothly, contributing to the overall stability and continuity of the cosmic order.

Shesha's Connection with Major Deities

1. Shesha and Vishnu:

Shesha is closely associated with **Vishnu**, one of the principal deities in Hinduism. Vishnu is often depicted reclining on Shesha, symbolizing his dependence on the cosmic serpent for support. This depiction highlights Shesha's role as a foundational element in the divine realm, with Vishnu representing the principle of preservation and stability in the cosmos. Shesha's support of Vishnu signifies his essential role in sustaining the divine order and ensuring the protection of the universe.

2. Shesha and Brahma:

While Vishnu is primarily associated with Shesha, the serpent also has connections to **Brahma**, the creator deity. According to certain texts, Brahma emerges from the navel of Vishnu, who rests upon Shesha. This connection reinforces Shesha's role as a fundamental support in the cosmic process, facilitating the creation and sustenance of the universe.

3. Shesha and Shiva:

In some traditions, Shesha is also linked to **Shiva**, the deity of destruction and transformation. The serpent's role in cosmic dissolution and renewal aligns with Shiva's functions in the cycle of creation and destruction. Shesha's association with Shiva highlights the interconnectedness of the cosmic forces and the serpent's role in maintaining the balance between creation, preservation, and destruction.

The Cosmic Significance of Shesha's Support

1. Balance and Harmony:

Shesha's role as the cosmic support structure is crucial for maintaining balance and harmony in the universe. His presence ensures that all realms and elements of the cosmos function in their intended order. By upholding the universe, Shesha contributes to the overall stability and equilibrium of the cosmic system.

2. The Cyclical Nature of the Cosmos:

The cyclical nature of the universe, including processes of creation, preservation, and dissolution, is reflected in Shesha's role. His support during these cycles ensures that the cosmic order is maintained and that the universe undergoes its transformations in a harmonious and balanced manner.

3. The Interconnection of Cosmic Realms:

Shesha's function as the cosmic serpent emphasizes the interconnectedness of various cosmic realms. His support of Vishnu, Brahma, and Shiva underscores the unity of divine forces and the seamless operation of the cosmic system. Shesha's role highlights the interdependence of different aspects of the universe and the importance of maintaining a cohesive and balanced cosmic order.

Shesha in Rituals and Worship

1. Ritual Offerings to Shesha:

In Hindu rituals and worship, Shesha is honored through offerings and prayers that acknowledge his role as the cosmic support structure. Rituals may include offerings of serpentine symbols, precious materials, and sacred texts that reflect his connection to divine wealth and cosmic stability. These offerings seek blessings from Shesha for prosperity, protection, and the preservation of cosmic order.

2. Temples and Veneration:

Temples dedicated to Shesha or the Nagas often feature elaborate serpent iconography and serve as centers for worship and veneration. These temples may include depictions of Shesha in various forms, such as reclining on Vishnu or supporting cosmic realms. The worship of Shesha in these temples reflects his importance as a cosmic foundation and his role in maintaining the stability and harmony of the universe.

3. Festivals and Celebrations:

Festivals and celebrations related to Shesha may emphasize his role in upholding the cosmic order and preserving divine treasures. These events often involve rituals that seek to honor Shesha's guardianship and express gratitude for his role in maintaining cosmic balance. The celebration of Shesha's role underscores his continued relevance in contemporary spiritual practices.

Shesha's Role in Contemporary Context

1. Preservation of Tradition:

The traditional role of Shesha as a cosmic foundation continues to be recognized and honored in Hindu practices and cultural traditions. Rituals, festivals, and worship dedicated to Shesha maintain the relevance of his role in preserving ancient customs and beliefs. The preservation of these traditions reflects the ongoing importance of Shesha in Hindu cosmology.

2. Modern Interpretations:

Contemporary interpretations of Shesha's role may focus on his symbolic significance as a guardian of cosmic balance and stability. Modern discussions may explore how Shesha's role reflects broader themes of interconnectedness, continuity, and responsibility in both spiritual and worldly contexts. These interpretations highlight the enduring relevance of Shesha in contemporary spiritual thought.

3. Influence on Popular Culture:

The depiction of Shesha in popular culture, including literature, art, and media, reflects his enduring significance and appeal. Modern portrayals often blend traditional mythology with contemporary themes, making Shesha's role as a cosmic foundation accessible and engaging to a broader audience. The influence of Shesha in popular culture underscores his continued relevance and impact.

Conclusion

Shesha's role as the cosmic serpent and foundation represents a profound and multifaceted aspect of Hindu cosmology. His symbolism as a guardian of eternity, support structure, and transformative force highlights the deep interconnectedness of the universe and the importance of maintaining cosmic balance. Through his functions in creation, preservation, and dissolution, Shesha embodies the eternal nature of the cosmos and the seamless operation of divine forces.

As a central figure in Hindu thought, Shesha's role reflects the ongoing relevance of his guardianship and the timeless truths embodied in his serpentine form. His continued presence in rituals, worship, and contemporary interpretations underscores the enduring significance of Shesha in preserving the cosmic order and ensuring the stability and harmony of the universe.

- The Sacred Geometry of Shesha

Introduction

In the intricate tapestry of Hindu cosmology, the concept of **sacred geometry** plays a pivotal role in understanding the divine structure of the universe. **Shesha**, the cosmic serpent and embodiment of infinity, is intimately connected with sacred geometry, reflecting profound cosmic principles and spiritual truths. The sacred geometry associated with Shesha not only highlights his role as the foundational support of the cosmos but also embodies the harmony, balance, and continuity inherent in the universe. This chapter explores the sacred geometry of Shesha, delving into the symbolic and practical aspects of his geometric representation and its significance in Hindu thought.

Shesha and Sacred Geometry

1. The Infinite Coil:

Shesha's most striking geometric feature is his **endless coils**, which symbolize the infinite nature of time and existence. Each coil of Shesha represents an unbroken continuum, illustrating the concept of eternity and the cyclical nature of the universe. The visual of the serpent's coils reflects the idea that the universe is perpetually supported by an infinite, unbroken structure. This geometric representation underscores the eternal and boundless nature of the cosmos.

- **Symbolism of the Coil:** The coiled serpent symbolizes the cyclical processes of creation, preservation, and dissolution. Just as the serpent's coils are continuous, the universe undergoes endless cycles of transformation. The geometric pattern of these coils represents the seamless transition between different phases of cosmic activity, reflecting the dynamic yet harmonious nature of the universe.

2. The Cosmic Axis:

In Hindu cosmology, Shesha is often depicted as forming the **cosmic axis** or the central support of the universe. This axis can be envisioned as a vertical line that connects the different realms of existence—the heavens, earth, and underworld. The axis represents the structural integrity of the universe, with Shesha's body providing the central support around which the cosmic order revolves.

- **Symbolic Representation:** The cosmic axis symbolizes the axis mundi, or the world axis, which connects the divine and the earthly realms. Shesha's role as the axis reflects his function in maintaining the alignment and stability of the cosmic order. The vertical alignment of the axis represents the central point of cosmic balance and unity.

3. The Serpent's Mandala:

The geometric pattern formed by Shesha's body can be visualized as a **mandala**, a symbolic representation of the universe and its divine principles. In this context, the mandala represents the sacred, ordered structure of the cosmos, with Shesha as the central figure around which the divine order is organized.

- **Mandala Symbolism:** The mandala symbolizes the totality of the cosmos, encompassing both the material and spiritual realms. Shesha's form as a mandala reflects his role in maintaining the unity and harmony of the universe. The mandala's geometric precision represents the divine order and the perfect balance maintained by Shesha.

4. The Serpent's Spiral:

The **spiral** is another significant geometric pattern associated with Shesha. The spiral represents growth, evolution, and the unfolding of the cosmic order. Shesha's spiraling form embodies the dynamic and ever-evolving nature of the universe, with each spiral reflecting a phase of cosmic development or transformation.

- **Symbolic Meaning:** The spiral signifies the continuous process of creation and dissolution, reflecting the cyclical nature of existence. Shesha's spiraling coils represent the ever-changing yet eternal nature of the cosmos, highlighting the interplay between order and chaos, stability and dynamism.

Sacred Geometry in Hindu Texts and Iconography

1. Vedic and Puranic Descriptions:

In the **Vedas** and **Puranas**, Shesha's geometric symbolism is often described in abstract terms, focusing on his role as a cosmic support. The texts highlight his function in upholding the universe and maintaining cosmic balance, with less emphasis on explicit geometric representations. However, the underlying principles of sacred geometry are present in the descriptions of Shesha's role and function.

- **Vedic Texts:** The Vedic texts mention cosmic serpents and primordial deities, laying the groundwork for the concept of sacred geometry associated with Shesha. The descriptions of Shesha's support and stability reflect the underlying geometric principles of balance and continuity.
- **Puranic Texts:** The Puranas provide more detailed accounts of Shesha's role in cosmic events, such as the churning of the ocean (Samudra Manthan). These texts illustrate Shesha's geometric function in supporting the cosmic process and maintaining the divine order.

2. Iconographic Representation:

In Hindu iconography, Shesha is often depicted with geometric precision, reflecting his role as the cosmic serpent. The visual representation of Shesha's coils, spirals, and mandalas embodies the sacred geometry associated with his role as the cosmic foundation.

- **Iconographic Details:** The depiction of Shesha with multiple coils and intricate patterns highlights the geometric principles of infinity and balance. The alignment and arrangement of Shesha's form in iconographic representations reflect the divine order and harmony maintained by the serpent.

3. Rituals and Sacred Architecture:

Sacred geometry associated with Shesha is also reflected in Hindu rituals and temple architecture. Temples dedicated to Shesha or the Nagas often feature geometric patterns and mandalas that embody the cosmic principles associated with the serpent.

- **Temple Architecture:** The design and layout of temples dedicated to Shesha incorporate geometric patterns and sacred symbols, reflecting his role as the cosmic support structure. The architecture of these temples aligns with the principles of sacred geometry, emphasizing the connection between the divine and the material realms.
- **Ritual Practices:** Rituals and offerings dedicated to Shesha may involve geometric symbols and patterns, reflecting his role in maintaining cosmic balance. The use of sacred geometry in rituals underscores the importance of Shesha's guardianship and the divine order.

The Cosmic Implications of Shesha's Geometry

1. The Harmony of the Universe:

The sacred geometry associated with Shesha reflects the inherent harmony and balance of the cosmos. His endless coils, cosmic axis, mandala, and spiral patterns represent the ordered structure of the universe and the seamless integration of divine principles. Shesha's geometric symbolism underscores the interconnectedness of all cosmic elements and the stability maintained by the serpent.

2. The Continuity of Cosmic Processes:

Shesha's geometry highlights the continuity and cyclical nature of cosmic processes. The serpent's coils and spirals represent the unbroken flow of time and existence, reflecting the perpetual cycles of creation, preservation, and dissolution. Shesha's geometric form embodies the eternal and dynamic nature of the universe.

3. The Divine Order and Structure:

The geometric patterns associated with Shesha symbolize the divine order and structure of the cosmos. His role as the cosmic serpent reflects the principles of balance, stability, and harmony maintained by the divine forces. Shesha's geometry represents the perfect alignment and integration of cosmic elements, emphasizing the unity and coherence of the universe.

Shesha's Sacred Geometry in Contemporary Context

1. Modern Interpretations:

Contemporary interpretations of Shesha's sacred geometry often explore the symbolic significance of his geometric patterns in relation to modern concepts of balance, harmony, and cosmic order. The principles of sacred geometry associated with Shesha continue to inspire discussions on the interconnectedness of the universe and the role of divine forces in maintaining cosmic stability.

2. Influence on Art and Design:

The geometric patterns associated with Shesha have influenced art and design, both in traditional and contemporary contexts. The visual representation of Shesha's geometry can be seen in various forms of artistic expression, including mandalas, sculptures, and architectural designs. These influences highlight the enduring impact of Shesha's sacred geometry on creative and spiritual practices.

3. Educational and Spiritual Insights:

The study of Shesha's sacred geometry provides valuable insights into the cosmic principles and spiritual truths embodied by the serpent. Educational and spiritual discussions on Shesha's geometry offer a deeper understanding of the divine order and the interconnectedness of the universe. These insights contribute to a broader appreciation of Hindu cosmology and the significance of sacred geometry.

Conclusion

The sacred geometry of Shesha represents a profound and multifaceted aspect of Hindu cosmology. His endless coils, cosmic axis, mandala, and spiral patterns embody the principles of infinity, balance, and harmony inherent in the universe. Through his geometric symbolism, Shesha reflects the ordered structure and continuous processes that sustain the cosmic order.

As a central figure in Hindu thought, Shesha's sacred geometry underscores the interconnectedness of divine and material realms, emphasizing the stability and unity maintained by the cosmic serpent. The continued exploration and interpretation of Shesha's geometry highlight the enduring significance of sacred geometry in understanding the divine principles and cosmic structure that shape the universe.

- Shesha and the Multiverse

Introduction

The concept of the **multiverse**, an intricate tapestry of multiple, interconnected universes or realms, has gained considerable attention in contemporary scientific and philosophical discourse. Within the rich tapestry of Hindu cosmology, this concept finds resonance in the divine figure of **Shesha**, the cosmic serpent who serves as the foundation and support of the universe. Shesha's role transcends the boundaries of a single universe, reflecting a profound understanding of the multiverse as an interconnected, infinite continuum. This chapter delves into the multifaceted relationship between Shesha and the multiverse, exploring how this cosmic entity embodies the principles of multiversal existence and contributes to the intricate structure of the divine cosmos.

Shesha as the Foundation of the Multiverse

1. The Infinite Cosmic Serpent:

Shesha, also known as Adishesha, is often depicted as an infinitely coiled serpent, symbolizing the boundless and unending nature of the cosmos. His infinite coils represent not only the continuity of time but also the existence of multiple realms or universes within the cosmic structure. Shesha's role as the cosmic serpent aligns with the concept of the multiverse, where he serves as the foundational support for an infinite array of universes.

- **Symbolism of Infinity:** The infinite coils of Shesha embody the idea that the cosmos extends beyond a single universe into a vast multiversal expanse. His form as an unending serpent reflects the limitless nature of existence, accommodating the concept of multiple, parallel, and interconnected universes.

2. Shesha's Role in Cosmic Support:

In Hindu cosmology, Shesha is described as supporting the **earth** and various realms, including the underworld and the celestial spheres. This support extends beyond a singular universe to encompass a broader multiversal framework. Shesha's role as a cosmic support underscores the idea that he upholds not just one, but a multitude of universes, each existing in a complex network of divine order.

- **Cosmic Support Across Realms:** Shesha's function in supporting multiple realms highlights his role in maintaining the stability and interconnectedness of the multiverse. His support is not limited to a single plane of existence but extends to the entirety of the cosmic structure, reflecting the interdependence of various universes within the multiverse.

3. The Cosmic Axis and Multiversal Connectivity:

The concept of the **cosmic axis**, often associated with Shesha, can be envisioned as a central support that connects various realms or universes within the multiverse. This axis serves as a conduit through which the different universes are linked, maintaining the harmony and balance of the entire multiversal structure.

- **Symbolic Axis:** The cosmic axis represents the central point around which the multiverse is organized. Shesha's role in maintaining this axis underscores his function in connecting and aligning the multiple realms of existence. The axis serves as the divine connector that integrates the various universes into a cohesive whole.

Shesha and the Cosmic Order

1. The Role of Shesha in Creation and Dissolution:

Shesha's involvement in the processes of **creation** and **dissolution** is crucial to understanding his relationship with the multiverse. In Hindu cosmology, Shesha plays a significant role in the cyclical processes of cosmic creation and dissolution, which extend to the multiversal level. His presence during these processes reflects the dynamic nature of the multiverse, where universes are continually created, sustained, and dissolved.

- **Creation and Dissolution Cycles:** Shesha's role in supporting Vishnu during the **creation** and **dissolution** of the universe highlights his involvement in the broader cycles of the multiverse. These cycles illustrate the dynamic and ever-changing nature of the multiverse, with Shesha acting as a constant support throughout the process.

2. The Preservation of Cosmic Balance:

Shesha's role in maintaining **cosmic balance** is vital to the stability of the multiverse. As the cosmic serpent, Shesha ensures that the various realms and universes remain in harmony, preventing chaos and disorder. His presence represents the divine order that governs the entire multiversal structure, ensuring the stability and interconnectedness of the different universes.

- **Balance and Harmony:** Shesha's function in preserving cosmic balance underscores his importance in maintaining the overall structure of the multiverse. His support ensures that the multiple realms and universes coexist in a state of equilibrium, reflecting the divine order that pervades the multiversal system.

The Multiverse in Hindu Texts

1. Vedic and Puranic References:

In the **Vedas** and **Puranas**, the concept of the multiverse is indirectly referenced through descriptions of various realms, dimensions, and cosmic entities. While these texts may not explicitly outline a multiverse in modern terms, they provide insights into the complex and interconnected nature of the cosmos, with Shesha playing a significant role in this structure.

- **Vedic Descriptions:** The Vedic texts describe multiple realms and dimensions, suggesting a complex cosmological structure that aligns with the idea of a multiverse. Shesha's role in supporting these realms reflects his importance in maintaining the order and stability of the entire cosmic system.
- **Puranic Accounts:** The Puranas provide more detailed accounts of Shesha's role in the cosmic structure, including his support for various realms and his involvement in cosmic events. These texts highlight Shesha's significance in the broader context of the multiverse, emphasizing his role as a foundational support for multiple universes.

2. Iconographic Depictions:

In Hindu iconography, Shesha is often depicted with multiple coils and complex patterns, reflecting the vastness and complexity of the multiverse. His form represents the intricate and interconnected nature of the cosmic structure, with each coil symbolizing a different aspect or realm of the multiverse.

- **Visual Representation:** The iconographic depiction of Shesha with his coils and patterns illustrates the expansive nature of the multiverse. Each coil represents a different universe or realm, highlighting the interconnectedness and diversity of the cosmic structure.

3. Rituals and Cosmological Practices:

Rituals and practices dedicated to Shesha often incorporate elements that reflect the multiversal concept. The use of sacred geometry, symbolic patterns, and ritualistic elements represents the interconnected nature of the cosmos and the role of Shesha in maintaining the balance of the multiverse.

- **Ritual Symbolism:** The rituals and practices dedicated to Shesha often involve geometric patterns and symbols that represent the multiverse. These elements emphasize the divine order and interconnectedness of the various realms and universes.

The Multiverse and Contemporary Understanding

1. Modern Scientific Perspectives:

The concept of the multiverse has gained traction in modern scientific theories, particularly in cosmology and quantum physics. While these theories differ from traditional Hindu cosmology, they align with the idea of multiple, interconnected universes. Shesha's role as the cosmic serpent reflects similar principles of interconnectedness and infinite existence.

- **Scientific Theories:** Modern scientific theories on the multiverse propose the existence of multiple universes with their own distinct properties and laws. These theories resonate with the concept of a vast, interconnected cosmic structure, reflecting the principles embodied by Shesha in Hindu cosmology.

2. Philosophical and Spiritual Implications:

The exploration of Shesha's role in the multiverse offers philosophical and spiritual insights into the nature of existence and the divine order. The concept of a multiverse challenges conventional notions of reality and emphasizes the interconnectedness of all realms, reflecting the profound spiritual truths associated with Shesha.

- **Philosophical Insights:** The idea of a multiverse challenges our understanding of reality and existence, offering new perspectives on the nature of the cosmos. Shesha's role as a cosmic support and foundation aligns with these insights, emphasizing the interconnected and divine nature of the multiversal structure.

3. The Future of Multiversal Exploration:

As our understanding of the multiverse continues to evolve, the exploration of Shesha's role provides valuable insights into the cosmic principles and spiritual truths associated with this concept. The ongoing study of Shesha and the multiverse offers opportunities for deeper exploration and integration of ancient wisdom with modern scientific and philosophical perspectives.

- **Future Research:** The study of Shesha's role in the multiverse contributes to a broader understanding of cosmic principles and the interconnected nature of existence. Future research may further elucidate the relationship between ancient cosmological concepts and contemporary scientific theories, enhancing our appreciation of the divine order and the multiversal structure.

Conclusion

The relationship between Shesha and the multiverse reflects a profound understanding of cosmic structure and divine order. Shesha's role as the cosmic serpent, with his infinite coils and foundational support, embodies the principles of multiversal existence, interconnectedness, and eternal continuity. His presence underscores the complexity and harmony of the cosmic system, offering insights into the nature of reality and the divine principles that govern the multiverse.

As we explore the concept of the multiverse in both traditional and contemporary contexts, Shesha's role provides a valuable perspective on the infinite and interconnected nature of existence. The study of Shesha and the multiverse highlights the enduring significance of ancient cosmological concepts and their relevance to modern scientific and philosophical inquiries, offering a deeper appreciation of the divine order and the vastness of the cosmic structure.

Chapter 9: Shesha and the Mystical Serpents of Other Cultures

- Serpent Symbolism Across the World

Introduction

The serpent, a creature revered and feared throughout human history, occupies a unique and multifaceted role across various cultures and mythologies. As a symbol of transformation, immortality, and divine power, serpents have woven themselves into the spiritual and mythological fabric of civilizations worldwide. Among these serpents, **Shesha** stands out in Hindu cosmology as the cosmic serpent who supports the universe and embodies the principles of eternity and divine order. This chapter explores the symbolism of serpents across different cultures, examining how these symbols resonate with and diverge from the role of Shesha in Hindu tradition.

The Universal Symbolism of Serpents

1. Serpent as a Symbol of Immortality and Renewal:

In many cultures, the serpent is associated with themes of **immortality** and **renewal**. This symbolism often stems from the serpent's ability to shed its skin, representing rebirth and the cyclical nature of life.

- **Greek Mythology:** In Greek mythology, the serpent is linked with the god **Asclepius**, who was associated with healing and medicine. The **Rod of Asclepius**, a staff with a serpent coiled around it, symbolizes regeneration and healing. The serpent's shedding of its skin is seen as a metaphor for renewal and transformation, echoing the regenerative aspects seen in the serpent symbolism in other cultures.

- **Ancient Egypt:** The **Uraeus** serpent in ancient Egyptian iconography represents the goddess **Wadjet** and symbolizes divine authority and protection. The Uraeus often adorns the crowns of pharaohs, signifying their role as eternal rulers and their divine right to govern. The serpent's cyclical shedding of skin reflects the eternal nature of the divine and the endless cycle of life and rebirth.

2. Serpent as a Guardian and Protector:

Serpents are frequently depicted as guardians and protectors of sacred spaces, treasures, and knowledge, reflecting their role as intermediaries between the human and divine realms.

- **Greek Mythology:** The serpent **Python** guarded the oracle of Delphi, symbolizing the protection of sacred knowledge and divine wisdom. Python's role as a guardian emphasizes the serpent's association with sacred spaces and the protection of divine truths.
- **Mesopotamian Mythology:** In Mesopotamian myth, the serpent **Tiamat** is a primordial deity who embodies chaos and the saltwater ocean. Her form as a serpent reflects her role as a guardian of the chaotic primordial waters, which are essential for the creation and maintenance of the cosmos.

3. Serpent as a Symbol of Wisdom and Knowledge:

The serpent is often associated with wisdom, knowledge, and the pursuit of enlightenment, reflecting its role as a symbol of deep, esoteric understanding.

- **Judeo-Christian Tradition:** In the Judeo-Christian tradition, the serpent in the Garden of Eden is a symbol of knowledge and temptation. Although it is often depicted as a deceiver, the serpent's role in introducing knowledge to humanity reflects its association with enlightenment and the quest for understanding.
- **Chinese Mythology:** In Chinese tradition, the **dragon**, a serpentine creature, symbolizes wisdom, power, and the harmony of the cosmos. The dragon's association with imperial authority and divine wisdom highlights the serpent's role as a bearer of profound knowledge and spiritual insight.

Shesha and Serpentine Symbolism in Hinduism

1. Shesha as the Cosmic Foundation:

In Hinduism, Shesha, or **Adishesha**, is the primordial serpent who supports the universe and represents the infinite cosmic order. His role as the cosmic serpent aligns with the broader symbolism of serpents as foundational beings within the cosmic structure.

- **Support of Vishnu:** Shesha serves as the divine support for Vishnu, the preserver of the universe, reflecting his role as a stabilizing force within the cosmos. Shesha's support of Vishnu underscores his importance as a guardian of the divine order and protector of cosmic stability.
- **Infinite Coils:** Shesha's depiction with infinite coils symbolizes the boundless nature of the cosmos and the endless cycles of time and creation. This imagery resonates with the universal symbolism of the serpent as a representation of infinity and eternal renewal.

2. Shesha and the Divine Cosmic Order:

Shesha's role in maintaining the divine cosmic order aligns with the broader serpent symbolism seen in other cultures, where serpents are often depicted as guardians of sacred order and divine balance.

- **Support During Pralaya:** During the cosmic dissolution (Pralaya), Shesha plays a crucial role in supporting Vishnu and preserving the cosmic order. His function during these periods highlights his role as a protector and sustainer of divine balance, similar to the serpent guardianship seen in other mythologies.

- **Role in Creation:** Shesha's involvement in the creation of the universe reflects his role as a foundational figure who supports and sustains the divine process of cosmic genesis. His contribution to creation aligns with the serpent symbolism of bringing forth life and maintaining the cosmic order.

Serpents in Other Cultural Mythologies

1. Aztec and Mesoamerican Cultures:

In Aztec and Mesoamerican cultures, the serpent is a prominent symbol associated with fertility, agriculture, and the underworld. The **feathered serpent god Quetzalcoatl** represents a blend of serpent and bird symbolism, embodying both the celestial and terrestrial aspects of existence.

- **Quetzalcoatl:** Quetzalcoatl, the feathered serpent, symbolizes the integration of earth and sky, reflecting the serpent's role as a bridge between different realms of existence. His association with fertility and creation highlights the serpent's role in sustaining and nurturing life.

2. Native American Cultures:

In various Native American traditions, serpents are often seen as symbols of earth and water, embodying the cyclical nature of life and the connection between the physical and spiritual worlds.

- **The Rainbow Serpent:** In Australian Aboriginal mythology, the Rainbow Serpent is a creator deity associated with water and the land. The serpent's role in shaping the landscape and bringing forth life emphasizes its significance as a powerful and transformative force within the natural world.

3. African Mythologies:

In African mythologies, serpents are often revered as symbols of fertility, wisdom, and the divine. The **serpent deity Damballa** in the Vodou tradition represents creation, life, and the connection between the physical and spiritual realms.

- **Damballa:** Damballa, the serpent deity in Vodou, is associated with creation and the life-giving properties of water. His role as a divine being who connects the physical and spiritual realms reflects the broader symbolism of serpents as intermediaries between different planes of existence.

Comparative Analysis

1. Common Themes and Divergences:

Across different cultures, serpents share common themes of immortality, renewal, protection, and wisdom. These themes resonate with the role of Shesha in Hindu cosmology, where he serves as the cosmic serpent who upholds the universe and maintains divine order. However, variations in symbolism and mythological roles reflect the unique cultural contexts in which these serpents are revered.

- **Common Themes:** The symbolism of immortality, renewal, and cosmic support is prevalent across various cultures, highlighting the universal reverence for serpents as embodiments of divine principles and cosmic forces.

- **Cultural Variations:** While common themes exist, cultural variations in serpent symbolism reflect diverse mythological and spiritual contexts. Each culture's interpretation of serpents provides insights into their understanding of the cosmos and the divine.

2. Shesha's Role in the Global Context:

Shesha's role as the cosmic serpent within Hindu cosmology can be understood in relation to the broader global context of serpent symbolism. His functions as a protector, support for the divine order, and embodiment of infinity align with universal themes seen in other cultural traditions.

- **Global Reverence:** The global reverence for serpents reflects their significance as symbols of profound spiritual truths and cosmic principles. Shesha's role in Hinduism mirrors these themes, emphasizing his importance as a foundational and divine being within the cosmic structure.

Conclusion

The exploration of serpent symbolism across various cultures reveals a rich and complex tapestry of meanings and roles. From ancient Egypt to Mesoamerica, serpents are revered as symbols of immortality, renewal, wisdom, and divine protection. Shesha, as the cosmic serpent in Hindu cosmology, embodies these universal themes, representing the eternal support and maintenance of the divine order.

As we compare Shesha's role with serpentine symbols in other cultures, we gain a deeper understanding of the serpent's significance in the global context. The shared themes of immortality, renewal, and cosmic support highlight the serpent's enduring role as a symbol of divine principles and cosmic forces. Through this comparative analysis, we appreciate the universal reverence for serpents and the profound spiritual truths they represent in diverse cultural traditions.

- Shesha and the Kundalini Energy

Introduction

In the vast and intricate landscape of Hindu spirituality, the concept of **Kundalini** energy holds a central place, symbolizing the dormant spiritual potential within every individual. This latent energy, often visualized as a coiled serpent, mirrors the image of **Shesha**, the cosmic serpent, whose role in Hindu cosmology extends beyond the physical realm into the spiritual and metaphysical dimensions. This chapter delves into the profound connections between Shesha and Kundalini energy, exploring how the symbolism and function of Shesha reflect the esoteric principles of Kundalini and its transformative power.

Understanding Kundalini Energy

1. The Concept of Kundalini:

Kundalini, derived from the Sanskrit word meaning "coiled," represents a form of primal energy believed to reside at the base of the spine, in the **Muladhara** (root) chakra. This energy, when awakened, rises through the **sushumna nadi** (central energy channel) along the spine, activating the seven primary chakras and leading to spiritual enlightenment and self-realization.

- **Spiritual Potential:** Kundalini is considered a latent spiritual potential that, when awakened, facilitates profound personal and spiritual transformation. The awakening of Kundalini is said to bring about increased awareness, heightened perception, and a deep connection with the divine.

- **Transformation and Enlightenment:** The process of awakening Kundalini involves the gradual opening of the chakras and the expansion of consciousness. This transformative journey is believed to lead to a state of enlightenment, where the individual experiences unity with the divine and a profound sense of inner peace.

2. The Symbolism of the Coiled Serpent:

The serpent imagery used to represent Kundalini is not merely a symbolic choice but a reflection of the serpent's inherent qualities of energy, transformation, and awakening. The coiled serpent symbolizes the dormant potential that resides within, waiting to be awakened and integrated into the spiritual journey.

- **Dormancy and Potential:** The coiled form of the serpent represents the latent energy that lies dormant at the base of the spine. This coiling symbolizes potential energy that is waiting to be activated and harnessed through spiritual practice.
- **Rising Energy:** As the serpent uncoils and rises, it mirrors the ascent of Kundalini through the chakras, symbolizing the process of spiritual awakening and the integration of higher consciousness.

Shesha and Kundalini: Parallels and Connections

1. Shesha as the Cosmic Serpent:

Shesha, also known as Adishesha, is a primordial serpent in Hindu cosmology who supports the universe and serves as the divine foundation. His role extends beyond the physical realm into the metaphysical, where he embodies principles of infinity, stability, and cosmic order.

- **Support of Vishnu:** Shesha supports Vishnu, the preserver of the universe, reflecting his role as a stabilizing force within the cosmos. This function parallels the role of Kundalini in supporting and elevating the spiritual energy of the individual.
- **Infinite Coils:** Shesha's depiction with multiple, infinite coils symbolizes the boundless nature of the universe and the cyclical nature of time. This imagery resonates with the concept of Kundalini energy, which is also depicted as coiled and infinite, representing the endless potential for spiritual growth and transformation.

2. Shesha's Symbolic Role in Spiritual Awakening:

The role of Shesha in maintaining cosmic order and supporting divine entities mirrors the transformative and stabilizing effects of awakened Kundalini energy in an individual's spiritual journey.

- **Cosmic Stability:** Just as Shesha upholds the universe and maintains its stability, awakened Kundalini energy is believed to bring about a sense of inner stability and balance, aligning the individual with higher spiritual truths and cosmic principles.
- **Transformation and Unity:** Shesha's role in the cosmic process reflects the transformative journey that Kundalini represents. As Shesha supports and sustains the universe, awakened Kundalini facilitates the transformation of consciousness, leading to a unified experience of the divine.

The Process of Kundalini Awakening and Shesha's Influence

1. The Awakening of Kundalini:

The awakening of Kundalini involves a gradual and intentional process of spiritual practice, including meditation, yoga, and self-discipline. This process leads to the activation of the chakras and the ascent of energy through the sushumna nadi.

- **Spiritual Practices:** Practices such as **Kundalini yoga**, **pranayama** (breath control), and **meditation** are designed to awaken and guide the Kundalini energy. These practices help in aligning the individual's energy with the higher spiritual realms and facilitating the rise of consciousness.
- **Activation of Chakras:** As Kundalini rises through the chakras, it activates and balances each energy center, leading to enhanced spiritual insight, emotional healing, and a deeper connection with the divine.

2. Shesha's Role in Guiding Energy Flow:

Shesha's symbolism as the cosmic serpent aligns with the guidance and control of the Kundalini energy. Just as Shesha supports Vishnu and maintains cosmic order, the awakened Kundalini energy, when properly guided, leads to a harmonious and transformative spiritual experience.

- **Guidance and Stability:** Shesha's role in maintaining cosmic stability reflects the importance of guidance and stability in the process of Kundalini awakening. Proper guidance ensures that the awakening process is safe, balanced, and aligned with higher spiritual goals.
- **Integration of Higher Consciousness:** Shesha's function as a supporter of divine order parallels the integration of higher consciousness achieved through Kundalini awakening. Both represent a process of aligning with and embodying divine principles and spiritual truths.

The Metaphysical Dimensions of Shesha and Kundalini

1. Shesha and the Infinite Nature of Kundalini:

The infinite coils of Shesha symbolize the boundless nature of the cosmos, reflecting the limitless potential of Kundalini energy. This connection highlights the profound and infinite possibilities that arise from spiritual awakening and the integration of divine consciousness.

- **Eternal Cycle:** Shesha's role in the eternal cycle of creation and dissolution reflects the cyclical nature of Kundalini energy, which moves through cycles of awakening and integration. This cyclical process mirrors the cosmic cycles of creation, preservation, and dissolution.
- **Boundless Potential:** The boundless coils of Shesha symbolize the infinite potential for spiritual growth and transformation that Kundalini represents. This potential is realized through the awakening process, leading to a deeper connection with the divine and an expanded state of consciousness.

2. The Role of Shesha in Spiritual Ascension:

Shesha's support of Vishnu and his role in maintaining cosmic order reflect the principles of spiritual ascension and the attainment of higher states of consciousness through Kundalini awakening.

- **Divine Support:** Just as Shesha supports Vishnu in maintaining cosmic order, the awakened Kundalini energy supports the individual's spiritual journey, leading to the realization of divine truths and the attainment of higher states of consciousness.
- **Alignment with the Divine:** Shesha's function as a divine supporter and protector aligns with the goal of Kundalini awakening, which is to achieve a state of unity with the divine and a profound sense of inner peace and enlightenment.

Comparative Perspectives: Shesha and Kundalini in Global Contexts

1. Serpent Symbolism in Global Traditions:

The symbolism of serpents as coiled beings, representing latent energy and potential, is a common theme across various global traditions. This symbolism aligns with the depiction of Kundalini energy and Shesha in Hindu cosmology.

- **Global Symbolism:** The coiled serpent imagery used to represent latent energy and potential is found in various cultures, reflecting a universal understanding of the serpent as a symbol of transformation and spiritual awakening.
- **Cross-Cultural Parallels:** The parallels between Shesha and Kundalini energy in Hinduism and similar symbols in other cultures highlight a shared recognition of the serpent as a powerful symbol of spiritual potential and divine transformation.

2. Integration of Serpentine Symbols in Spiritual Practices:

The integration of serpentine symbols in spiritual practices across different cultures reflects a universal acknowledgment of the transformative power of these symbols. This integration provides insights into the global significance of Shesha and Kundalini energy.

- **Spiritual Practices:** The use of serpentine symbols in spiritual practices, such as meditation and energy work, underscores the importance of these symbols in guiding and facilitating spiritual growth and transformation.
- **Universal Significance:** The widespread presence of serpentine symbols in spiritual traditions highlights the universal significance of the serpent as a symbol of divine energy, transformation, and enlightenment.

Conclusion

The exploration of Shesha and Kundalini energy reveals profound connections between the cosmic serpent of Hindu cosmology and the esoteric principles of spiritual awakening. Shesha's role as the cosmic serpent who supports the universe and embodies the infinite nature of existence mirrors the transformative power of Kundalini energy, which represents the latent spiritual potential within every individual.

By understanding the parallels between Shesha and Kundalini, we gain insights into the universal symbolism of serpents as symbols of divine energy, transformation, and spiritual potential. This comparative perspective highlights the global significance of serpentine symbols and their role in guiding and facilitating spiritual growth and enlightenment.

Through this exploration, we appreciate the depth and complexity of Shesha's symbolism in Hindu cosmology and its resonance with the broader themes of spiritual awakening and divine transformation.

- Shesha in Buddhism and Jainism

Introduction

Shesha, the primordial serpent in Hindu mythology, is a figure of profound cosmic significance. In Hinduism, he represents the foundation of the universe, the support of Vishnu, and the eternal cycle of time. His presence is so pivotal that it transcends the boundaries of a single tradition. Not only does Shesha appear in various Hindu texts and practices, but his influence also extends into other major Indian religions, including **Buddhism** and **Jainism**. This chapter explores the role and symbolism of Shesha in these two traditions, analyzing how his representation aligns with and differs from his role in Hinduism.

Shesha in Buddhism

1. The Serpent Symbolism in Buddhism:

In Buddhism, serpents often appear in symbolism and iconography, though they are not always directly linked to Shesha. The **Nāgas**, which are serpent-like beings, play a significant role in Buddhist cosmology and mythology. While Nāgas are not identical to Shesha, they share several symbolic and functional similarities.

- **Nāgas and Their Attributes:** Nāgas are semi-divine beings, often depicted with the lower body of a serpent and the upper body of a human or a deity. They are associated with water, fertility, and protection. In Buddhist tradition, Nāgas are guardians of sacred sites and treasures, and they are believed to possess great spiritual and magical powers.

- **Symbolic Connections:** The serpent symbolism in Buddhism, represented by Nāgas, often aligns with the protective and transformative attributes of Shesha. Just as Shesha supports the cosmos and represents the eternal cycle, Nāgas are seen as protectors and custodians of spiritual knowledge and sacred spaces.

2. Shesha's Influence on Buddhist Texts:

While Shesha himself does not feature prominently in Buddhist texts, the concept of serpentine beings and their cosmic roles resonate with Buddhist ideas of protection, guardianship, and cosmic order.

- **The Serpent's Role in Buddhist Lore:** In the Pali Canon and other early Buddhist texts, Nāgas are described as beings who interact with the Buddha and his followers, often providing protection or assistance. For example, in the story of the Buddha's meditation under the **Bodhi tree**, a Nāga named **Mucalinda** protects him from a storm by wrapping around him with its hood.

- **Integration of Serpent Symbols:** Buddhist art and literature often depict Nāgas in contexts that echo the protective and foundational roles of Shesha. This integration reflects a shared understanding of the serpent as a powerful symbol of cosmic order and divine protection.

3. Comparative Symbolism:

In Buddhism, while Shesha's direct influence is minimal, the symbolism of serpents and their cosmic functions parallels the attributes assigned to Shesha in Hinduism.

- **Guardianship and Protection:** Both Shesha and Nāgas are associated with guardianship and protection. Shesha's role in supporting Vishnu and maintaining cosmic stability is mirrored in the Buddhist context where Nāgas guard sacred sites and spiritual treasures.
- **Transformation and Renewal:** The serpent symbolism in both traditions also emphasizes transformation and renewal. Shesha's role in the eternal cycle of time reflects the Buddhist concept of cycles of birth, death, and rebirth, where Nāgas are often seen as beings who help facilitate these processes.

Shesha in Jainism

1. Serpent Symbolism in Jain Cosmology:

In Jainism, serpents are less prominent than in Hinduism and Buddhism, but they still hold symbolic value. The Jain tradition incorporates serpentine symbolism in its cosmological and mythological framework, though Shesha himself does not appear explicitly in Jain texts.

- **Nāgas in Jainism:** Similar to Hinduism and Buddhism, Nāgas in Jainism are depicted as serpent-like beings, often associated with water and protection. They are considered guardian spirits of treasures and sacred knowledge.
- **Symbolic Resonance:** While Shesha is not a direct figure in Jainism, the symbolic attributes of serpents—such as their role in maintaining cosmic balance and their association with fertility and protection—resonate with Jain cosmological themes.

2. Jain Cosmology and Shesha's Attributes:

Jain cosmology emphasizes the importance of cosmic order and the cyclical nature of time, themes that align with Shesha's attributes in Hinduism.

- **Cosmic Support and Balance:** Jainism's view of the cosmos includes a detailed description of the universe's structure, including its divisions into various realms. While Jain texts do not mention Shesha, the principles of cosmic balance and stability that he represents are central to Jain cosmology, which emphasizes the orderly and harmonious structure of the universe.
- **The Role of Serpents:** In Jain texts, serpents are often associated with cosmic and protective roles. Their presence in Jain mythology reflects a similar function to Shesha, representing the maintenance of cosmic balance and the protection of sacred elements.

3. Comparative Perspectives:

Shesha's attributes in Hinduism, such as his role as a cosmic supporter and protector, have parallels in Jain cosmology and mythology.

- **Cosmic Order and Stability:** Both Hindu and Jain traditions emphasize the importance of maintaining cosmic order and stability. Shesha's role in supporting Vishnu and upholding the universe parallels the Jain focus on the balanced and orderly structure of the cosmos.

- **Symbolic Meanings:** The symbolism of serpents in Jainism, though not directly tied to Shesha, reflects similar themes of protection, balance, and divine guardianship. This shared symbolism underscores the cross-cultural resonance of serpent motifs in representing cosmic and spiritual principles.

Conclusion

Shesha's influence extends beyond Hinduism into the realms of Buddhism and Jainism, though his presence is more symbolic and indirect in these traditions. In Buddhism, the Nāgas share thematic similarities with Shesha, such as guardianship and cosmic order, while in Jainism, serpentine symbols align with concepts of cosmic balance and protection. By exploring Shesha's role and symbolism in these diverse traditions, we gain a deeper understanding of the universal themes associated with serpents and their significance in the broader Indian religious and philosophical context.

Chapter 10: The Eternal Legacy of Shesha

- Shesha's Role in the Modern World

Introduction

Shesha, the primordial serpent in Hindu mythology, is a figure of profound cosmic significance. His role as the eternal supporter of Vishnu and his embodiment of the infinite and cyclical nature of the universe have made him a symbol of stability, transformation, and divine order. As we navigate the complexities of the modern world, the symbolism and teachings associated with Shesha offer enduring insights and relevance. This chapter explores Shesha's role in contemporary society, examining how his ancient symbolism continues to inspire and influence various aspects of modern life, spirituality, and environmental consciousness.

Shesha's Symbolism in Contemporary Spirituality

1. The Concept of Cosmic Support and Stability:

In the fast-paced and often chaotic modern world, the themes of stability and support embodied by Shesha are more relevant than ever. His role as the cosmic serpent who supports the universe resonates with contemporary spiritual seekers who strive for inner balance and stability.

- **Inner Stability and Personal Growth:** Shesha's symbolism of cosmic support and stability reflects the modern quest for personal growth and emotional resilience. As individuals navigate the challenges of contemporary life, the idea of finding a solid foundation within oneself, akin to Shesha's role in upholding the universe, serves as a source of inspiration and strength.

- **Spiritual Practices:** The spiritual practices that draw from Shesha's symbolism, such as meditation and mindfulness, are increasingly popular in modern wellness movements. These practices help individuals cultivate a sense of inner stability and alignment with higher spiritual principles, echoing Shesha's role as a cosmic stabilizer.

2. The Eternal Cycle of Time and Transformation:

Shesha's representation of the eternal cycles of time and transformation provides valuable perspectives on the nature of change and renewal in the modern era.

- **Understanding Change:** The cyclical nature of Shesha's symbolism offers insights into the nature of change and transformation. In a world marked by rapid technological advancements and societal shifts, recognizing the cyclical patterns of life and embracing change as a part of a greater cosmic rhythm can help individuals navigate transitions with greater ease and acceptance.
- **Resilience and Adaptability:** Shesha's role in the eternal cycle underscores the importance of resilience and adaptability. By understanding that change is an inherent part of existence, individuals can develop a more flexible approach to life's challenges and uncertainties.

Shesha's Influence on Environmental Consciousness

1. The Symbolism of Serpents and Environmental Stewardship:

In modern times, Shesha's symbolism as a protector and supporter of the cosmic order can be interpreted as a call for environmental stewardship and ecological balance.

- **Guardianship of Nature:** Just as Shesha supports Vishnu and upholds the universe, modern environmental movements emphasize the need for humanity to act as stewards of the natural world. The symbolism of Shesha as a guardian and protector resonates with the growing awareness of our responsibility to preserve and protect the environment.
- **Balancing Ecosystems:** The concept of cosmic balance embodied by Shesha aligns with contemporary efforts to maintain ecological equilibrium. By recognizing the interconnectedness of all life forms and the importance of preserving natural habitats, we honor the principles of balance and harmony that Shesha represents.

2. Environmental Initiatives Inspired by Shesha's Symbolism:

The principles associated with Shesha can inspire various environmental initiatives and movements aimed at promoting sustainability and conservation.

- **Sustainable Practices:** The emphasis on balance and stability in Shesha's symbolism encourages the adoption of sustainable practices that minimize environmental impact and promote long-term ecological health. This includes efforts to reduce waste, conserve resources, and support renewable energy sources.
- **Cultural and Spiritual Advocacy:** Shesha's role in maintaining cosmic order can also inspire cultural and spiritual advocacy for environmental protection. By integrating environmental consciousness into spiritual practices and cultural values, we can foster a deeper appreciation for the natural world and its preservation.

Shesha's Legacy in Art and Literature

1. Representation in Modern Art and Media:

Shesha's symbolism has found its way into various forms of modern art and media, reflecting his enduring influence and relevance.

- **Artistic Depictions:** Contemporary artists often draw on Shesha's imagery to explore themes of cosmic order, transformation, and the infinite. These artistic representations serve as a bridge between ancient symbolism and modern creative expression, offering new interpretations and insights.
- **Literature and Popular Culture:** Shesha's presence in modern literature and popular culture underscores his continued relevance. His symbolism is often invoked in narratives that explore themes of cosmic balance, spiritual growth, and the eternal cycles of existence.

2. Educational and Cultural Projects:

Educational and cultural projects that focus on Shesha's symbolism contribute to a broader understanding of his role and significance.

- **Workshops and Seminars:** Educational initiatives that explore Shesha's symbolism provide opportunities for individuals to engage with his teachings and apply them to contemporary issues. Workshops and seminars can offer insights into the practical applications of Shesha's principles in daily life.
- **Cultural Celebrations:** Cultural events and celebrations that highlight Shesha's symbolism foster a deeper appreciation for his role in Hindu cosmology and promote cross-cultural understanding. These events can serve as platforms for exploring the intersections between ancient wisdom and modern values.

Shesha's Impact on Personal and Collective Consciousness

1. Personal Empowerment and Inner Transformation:

Shesha's symbolism offers valuable lessons for personal empowerment and inner transformation in the modern world.

- **Self-Discovery and Growth:** The themes of stability, support, and transformation associated with Shesha encourage individuals to embark on journeys of self-discovery and personal growth. By embracing the principles embodied by Shesha, individuals can cultivate a deeper sense of purpose and fulfillment.
- **Community and Connection:** Shesha's role as a cosmic supporter reflects the importance of community and interconnectedness. By fostering a sense of collective responsibility and mutual support, we can create more harmonious and compassionate communities.

2. Collective Consciousness and Global Awareness:

Shesha's legacy also extends to the realm of collective consciousness and global awareness.

- **Global Challenges:** The principles of cosmic balance and harmony embodied by Shesha offer guidance in addressing global challenges such as climate change, social inequality, and conflicts. By embracing these principles, we can work towards creating a more just and equitable world.
- **Interfaith and Cross-Cultural Dialogues:** Shesha's influence on spiritual and cultural traditions encourages interfaith and cross-cultural dialogues. By exploring the common themes and values

shared across different traditions, we can foster greater understanding and cooperation among diverse communities.

Conclusion

Shesha's role in the modern world is a testament to the enduring relevance of ancient symbolism and teachings. His representation as the cosmic serpent who supports the universe and embodies the eternal cycles of time offers valuable insights for contemporary life, spirituality, and environmental consciousness. By drawing on Shesha's legacy, we can navigate the complexities of the modern world with greater wisdom, resilience, and interconnectedness.

As we continue to explore and integrate the principles associated with Shesha, we honor his eternal legacy and embrace the timeless wisdom that he represents. Through personal empowerment, environmental stewardship, and collective consciousness, we can uphold the values embodied by Shesha and contribute to a more balanced and harmonious world.

- Lessons from Shesha's Life

Introduction

Shesha, the primordial serpent of Hindu cosmology, is not just a mythological figure but a symbol of profound cosmic truths and spiritual teachings. His life and role in various Hindu texts provide deep insights into the nature of existence, the cycles of time, and the principles of cosmic balance. Through an exploration of Shesha's life and attributes, we uncover timeless lessons that resonate with contemporary spiritual seekers and philosophers. This chapter delves into the key lessons derived from Shesha's life, examining their relevance and application in modern contexts.

1. The Principle of Cosmic Support and Stability

Shesha's Role as a Supporter:

One of the most fundamental aspects of Shesha's life is his role as the cosmic serpent who supports the universe. This principle highlights the importance of stability and support in maintaining cosmic order.

- **Symbolism of Support:** Shesha's function as a support for Vishnu during the cosmic dissolution underscores the necessity of a stable foundation in all aspects of existence. Just as Shesha upholds the universe, individuals and societies require stable support systems—be they in the form of relationships, institutions, or spiritual practices—to thrive and maintain balance.

- **Modern Relevance:** In contemporary life, the principle of support can be applied to personal and professional realms. Building and nurturing supportive relationships, creating resilient communities, and establishing dependable systems contribute to a sense of stability and well-being. Embracing the lessons of Shesha encourages individuals to be sources of support for others and to seek stability in their own lives.

2. Embracing the Eternal Cycles of Time

The Concept of Cycles:

Shesha's life is intrinsically tied to the cyclical nature of time and existence. His presence during the creation, preservation, and dissolution of the universe reflects the eternal cycles that govern cosmic processes.

- **Understanding Cycles:** The cyclical nature of Shesha's existence teaches us about the inevitability of change and the perpetual renewal of life. Recognizing that existence operates in cycles—be they daily, seasonal, or cosmic—can help individuals navigate periods of transformation with greater acceptance and resilience.
- **Application in Life:** Embracing the concept of cycles encourages a perspective of continuity and renewal. It teaches us to view challenges and transitions as natural phases in the broader cycle of existence. By understanding and accepting the cycles of life, individuals can approach change with a sense of purpose and adaptability.

3. The Power of Resilience and Adaptability

Shesha's Endurance:

Throughout Hindu mythology, Shesha's endurance and adaptability are highlighted. He remains steadfast in his role despite the cosmic upheavals and transformations that occur.

- **Resilience as a Virtue:** Shesha's unwavering presence during cosmic events demonstrates the value of resilience. His ability to adapt and persist through various phases of cosmic evolution serves as a model for personal resilience in the face of adversity.
- **Modern Implications:** In the modern world, resilience and adaptability are crucial qualities for navigating the complexities of life. Shesha's example inspires individuals to cultivate inner strength and flexibility, allowing them to respond effectively to challenges and uncertainties. By embracing resilience, individuals can overcome obstacles and continue their journey with determination and grace.

4. The Importance of Balance and Harmony

Shesha's Role in Cosmic Balance:

Shesha's role extends beyond mere support; he also embodies the principle of balance. His presence ensures the harmonious functioning of the universe, preventing chaos and maintaining order.

- **Principle of Balance:** The concept of balance is central to Shesha's life. His ability to maintain cosmic equilibrium amidst the ever-changing universe underscores the importance of harmony in all aspects of existence.
- **Contemporary Application:** Achieving balance in modern life involves managing various aspects—work, relationships, health, and spiritual practices—with mindfulness and intention. Shesha's lesson of balance encourages individuals to seek harmony within themselves and in their interactions with the world. By prioritizing balance, individuals can lead more fulfilling and harmonious lives.

5. The Value of Selflessness and Service

Shesha's Selfless Service:

Shesha's role as the supporter of Vishnu reflects a profound sense of selflessness and service. He remains dedicated to his cosmic duty without seeking personal gain or recognition.

- **Selflessness as a Path to Fulfillment:** Shesha's selfless service exemplifies the virtues of humility and devotion. His willingness to serve the divine purpose without expectation highlights the transformative power of selflessness.

- **Modern Practices:** In contemporary society, the value of selflessness and service can be integrated into daily life through acts of kindness, generosity, and compassion. Shesha's example encourages individuals to contribute to the well-being of others and to pursue a sense of purpose beyond personal interests. By embracing selflessness, individuals can experience deeper fulfillment and a sense of connection with the broader community.

6. The Interconnection of All Life Forms

Shesha's Cosmic Interconnection:

Shesha's existence underscores the interconnectedness of all life forms and cosmic elements. His role as a cosmic support highlights the interdependence between various aspects of the universe.

- **Understanding Interconnection:** Shesha's life illustrates the principle that all entities in the cosmos are interconnected and interdependent. This interconnectedness is essential for maintaining harmony and balance in the universe.

- **Contemporary Perspective:** Recognizing the interconnectedness of life encourages a holistic view of existence. In modern contexts, this understanding can inform environmental stewardship, social responsibility, and global cooperation. By acknowledging the interdependence of all life forms, individuals can work towards creating a more harmonious and sustainable world.

7. The Significance of Preservation and Protection

Shesha's Role in Preservation:

As the cosmic serpent, Shesha plays a crucial role in preserving the universe during periods of dissolution and transition. His function emphasizes the importance of preservation and protection in maintaining cosmic order.

- **Principle of Preservation:** Shesha's role in ensuring the stability and continuity of the cosmos highlights the significance of preservation. This principle extends to the safeguarding of natural resources, cultural heritage, and spiritual traditions.

- **Application in Modern Life:** In contemporary society, the value of preservation can be applied to environmental conservation, cultural preservation, and the protection of ethical values. Shesha's example inspires individuals to take proactive measures in safeguarding the planet and upholding values that contribute to the well-being of future generations.

8. The Journey of Self-Realization

Shesha's Symbolic Journey:

Shesha's life and role can be seen as a symbolic journey of self-realization and divine purpose. His unwavering support and stability reflect a profound understanding of his place in the cosmic order.

- **Path of Self-Realization:** The journey of Shesha symbolizes the quest for self-realization and understanding one's divine purpose. His steadfastness and dedication highlight the importance of aligning with one's true nature and purpose.
- **Modern Insights:** In the modern world, the journey of self-realization involves exploring one's values, passions, and spiritual goals. Shesha's life encourages individuals to embark on a path of self-discovery, aligning their actions with their higher purpose and contributing to the greater good.

Conclusion

The lessons derived from Shesha's life offer timeless insights into the nature of existence, cosmic order, and personal growth. His role as a supporter, symbol of cosmic balance, and embodiment of resilience and selflessness provides valuable guidance for contemporary life. By integrating these lessons into our daily practices, we honor Shesha's legacy and contribute to a more balanced, harmonious, and purposeful existence.

Shesha's life serves as a reminder of the enduring principles that govern the cosmos and the human experience. Through his example, we can navigate the complexities of modern life with greater wisdom, compassion, and understanding, drawing inspiration from the ancient teachings that continue to resonate in the present day.

- Shesha and the Future of Creation

Introduction

Shesha, the primordial serpent in Hindu cosmology, is a figure deeply intertwined with the cycles of creation, preservation, and dissolution. His role as the cosmic supporter of Vishnu and his embodiment of the infinite cycles of time make him a symbol of both the past and the future. As we contemplate the future of creation, Shesha's influence provides profound insights into the processes of cosmic renewal and transformation. This chapter explores how Shesha's symbolism and teachings can inform our understanding of the future of creation, offering a framework for envisioning the continued evolution of the cosmos and our place within it.

1. Shesha as a Symbol of Cosmic Renewal

The Cycles of Time and Creation:

Shesha's life is a testament to the cyclical nature of existence. His role in the cosmic cycles of creation, preservation, and dissolution reflects the eternal process of renewal that governs the universe.

- **Eternal Renewal:** The concept of cosmic renewal is central to Shesha's symbolism. His presence during the churning of the ocean (Samudra Manthan) and his support of Vishnu during cosmic dissolution emphasize the cyclical nature of creation. This cycle is not merely a repetitive process but a dynamic interplay of dissolution and rebirth that allows for continuous evolution and growth.

- **Future Implications:** As we look to the future, Shesha's role as a symbol of renewal suggests that creation will continue to evolve through cycles of transformation. Understanding this principle can help us embrace change as an integral part of the cosmic order and recognize that each phase of dissolution and rebirth contributes to the ongoing evolution of the universe.

2. Shesha and the Evolution of Cosmic Order

The Role of Shesha in Maintaining Cosmic Balance:

Shesha's role as the cosmic serpent who supports and upholds the universe underscores the importance of balance in the cosmic order. His influence extends to the future of creation, where maintaining balance and harmony will continue to be crucial.

- **Cosmic Equilibrium:** Shesha's function in maintaining cosmic equilibrium highlights the need for balance between opposing forces. In the future, this principle will be essential for sustaining harmony within the evolving universe. As new forms of existence emerge and old ones dissolve, the cosmic balance must be preserved to ensure the stability and coherence of the universe.

- **Guidance for the Future:** Shesha's example serves as a guide for maintaining balance in the face of change. By understanding the importance of equilibrium, we can approach the future with a commitment to harmony and stability, ensuring that our actions contribute positively to the ongoing evolution of creation.

3. Shesha's Influence on Spiritual Evolution

The Future of Spiritual Growth:

Shesha's symbolism extends beyond cosmic processes to the realm of spiritual evolution. His role in supporting Vishnu and embodying the eternal cycles of time offers valuable insights into the future of spiritual development.

- **Spiritual Continuity:** The concept of spiritual continuity is reflected in Shesha's role as a constant support for Vishnu. This continuity suggests that spiritual growth is an ongoing process that transcends individual lifetimes and extends into the future of creation. The principles of stability, resilience, and renewal associated with Shesha will continue to guide spiritual seekers as they navigate their journeys of self-realization.

- **Evolution of Spiritual Practices:** As humanity progresses, spiritual practices may evolve to reflect new understandings of existence and consciousness. Shesha's symbolism encourages an openness to this evolution while maintaining a connection to the timeless principles that underpin spiritual growth. By integrating these principles into modern practices, individuals can foster deeper spiritual connections and contribute to the collective evolution of consciousness.

4. The Role of Shesha in Environmental Stewardship

Sustaining the Cosmic Environment:

Shesha's connection to the cosmic order and his role in supporting Vishnu during periods of dissolution highlight the importance of environmental stewardship in the future of creation.

- **Ecological Balance:** Shesha's symbolism underscores the need for balance in the natural world. The principle of ecological balance, as embodied by Shesha, can guide efforts to preserve and protect the environment. Recognizing the interconnectedness of all life forms and the importance of maintaining natural harmony will be crucial for ensuring the sustainability of the cosmic environment.

- **Future Environmental Challenges:** As humanity faces increasing environmental challenges, Shesha's role as a guardian of cosmic order serves as a reminder of our responsibility to act as stewards of the Earth. By embracing practices that promote environmental sustainability and conservation, we can contribute to the preservation of the natural world and support the future of creation.

5. Shesha and the Integration of Science and Spirituality

Harmonizing Scientific and Spiritual Perspectives:

Shesha's role in the cosmic order highlights the potential for integrating scientific and spiritual perspectives in understanding the future of creation.

- **Scientific Discoveries and Spiritual Insights:** The exploration of cosmic processes and the nature of existence through science can complement spiritual insights. Shesha's symbolism provides a framework for harmonizing scientific discoveries with spiritual understanding, offering a more comprehensive view of the universe.

- **Future Innovations:** As scientific and technological advancements continue to shape the future, Shesha's principles of balance, renewal, and interconnectedness can guide the ethical and responsible application of these innovations. By integrating spiritual values into scientific progress, we can ensure that advancements contribute positively to the overall evolution of creation.

6. The Legacy of Shesha in Future Generations

Transmitting Wisdom to Future Generations:

Shesha's enduring legacy is a testament to the transmission of wisdom across generations. His role in the cosmic order provides valuable lessons for future generations.

- **Educational and Cultural Preservation:** The principles associated with Shesha—stability, renewal, balance, and interconnectedness—can be preserved and transmitted through education and cultural practices. By incorporating these values into educational curricula and cultural traditions, we can ensure that future generations are equipped with the wisdom to navigate the evolving cosmos.

- **Inspiring Future Leaders:** Shesha's example of selflessness, resilience, and cosmic support can inspire future leaders to approach their roles with a sense of purpose and responsibility. By embracing the lessons of Shesha, leaders can contribute to the harmonious development of society and the preservation of cosmic balance.

7. The Future Vision of Cosmic Harmony

Envisioning a Harmonious Future:

Shesha's role in maintaining cosmic harmony provides a vision for the future of creation, emphasizing the importance of unity and balance in the evolving universe.

- **Cosmic Unity:** The vision of cosmic unity, as reflected in Shesha's life, suggests that the future of creation will involve the continued integration of diverse elements into a cohesive whole. This vision encourages efforts to promote understanding, cooperation, and harmony among different cultures, communities, and belief systems.

- **Global and Universal Cooperation:** Embracing the principles of cosmic harmony can guide global and universal cooperation efforts. By working together towards common goals and fostering a sense of interconnectedness, we can contribute to the overall evolution of creation and support a more harmonious future.

Conclusion

Shesha's role in the cosmic order offers profound insights into the future of creation, highlighting the principles of renewal, balance, and interconnectedness. As we look ahead, the lessons derived from Shesha's life provide a framework for navigating the evolving cosmos with wisdom, resilience, and responsibility.

By embracing the principles embodied by Shesha—stability, adaptability, balance, and selflessness—we can contribute to the ongoing evolution of creation and ensure that the future is guided by the timeless wisdom of the cosmos. Shesha's legacy serves as a reminder of the enduring connection between the past, present, and future, offering a vision of harmony and renewal for generations to come.

Conclusion: The Infinite Protector

- The Final Vision of Shesha

As we draw our exploration of Shesha to a close, it is essential to reflect on the profound and multifaceted role this primordial serpent plays in the cosmic tapestry. Shesha, the infinite serpent, is not merely a character within Hindu mythology but a symbol of eternal cosmic principles and the ceaseless cycles of creation, preservation, and dissolution. His presence as the Infinite Protector embodies the essence of cosmic continuity and serves as a beacon of stability and renewal throughout the epochs.

1. Shesha as the Embodiment of Cosmic Stability

At the heart of Shesha's role lies his function as the embodiment of cosmic stability. His support for Vishnu, coiled around the divine and acting as his couch during the cosmic creation and dissolution, signifies the unwavering foundation upon which the universe rests. This stability is not static but dynamic, allowing for the perpetual motion of cosmic processes without losing its essence.

- **Cosmic Foundation:** Shesha's continuous presence throughout the yugas—Satya, Treta, Dvapara, and Kali—illustrates his role in maintaining the cosmic balance amidst the ever-changing cycles of time. His serpent form, representing both infinity and cyclicality, reinforces the idea that the universe is perpetually supported and rejuvenated.

- **Symbol of Resilience:** In the face of cosmic upheavals and transformations, Shesha remains a symbol of resilience and continuity. His ability to withstand the cataclysmic events of pralaya and re-emerge during the subsequent cycles highlights the inherent stability that underlies the seemingly chaotic nature of the universe.

2. The Vision of Eternal Renewal

Shesha's role extends beyond mere support to embody the principle of eternal renewal. The cyclical nature of the universe, characterized by the cycles of creation, preservation, and dissolution, is mirrored in Shesha's existence. His role in the Samudra Manthan, where he participates in the churning of the ocean to produce the nectar of immortality, underscores his integral involvement in the processes that sustain and renew life.

- **Cycle of Life and Death:** Shesha's participation in cosmic dissolution and rebirth reinforces the idea that life and death are interconnected aspects of a larger continuum. His symbolic presence ensures that even as individual entities undergo transformation, the overarching cosmic order remains intact and perpetually renewed.
- **Inspiration for Spiritual Growth:** Shesha's eternal nature serves as a metaphor for spiritual growth and evolution. His existence encourages individuals to view their spiritual journeys as part of a larger, cyclical process of self-realization and renewal, emphasizing that personal growth and transformation are part of the divine cosmic rhythm.

3. The Infinite Protector and the Future of Creation

Looking forward, Shesha's role as the Infinite Protector provides a guiding vision for the future of creation. His enduring presence suggests that the principles of stability, balance, and renewal will continue to shape the evolving cosmos.

- **Guiding Principles for the Future:** As humanity navigates the complexities of modern existence and faces global challenges, Shesha's principles offer a framework for addressing these issues with wisdom and resilience. Embracing the values of balance and interconnectedness can guide efforts towards sustainable development, environmental stewardship, and harmonious living.
- **Legacy of Cosmic Harmony:** Shesha's legacy as the Infinite Protector underscores the importance of maintaining cosmic harmony in all aspects of existence. By integrating the principles embodied by Shesha into our lives, we can contribute to a future that respects the cyclical nature of creation and fosters a sense of unity and balance.

4. Shesha's Influence on Spiritual and Cultural Practices

Shesha's influence extends beyond the realm of mythology into contemporary spiritual and cultural practices. His symbolism continues to inspire rituals, art, and philosophy, reflecting his enduring impact on human understanding of the cosmos.

- **Spiritual Inspiration:** The depiction of Shesha in spiritual practices and rituals serves as a reminder of the cosmic principles of balance and renewal. His representation in temples and iconography continues to inspire devotion and contemplation, offering a connection to the timeless wisdom of the universe.
- **Cultural Legacy:** Shesha's presence in cultural narratives and artistic expressions highlights the integration of cosmic principles into cultural traditions. His role as a symbol of infinite protection

and renewal enriches cultural practices and reinforces the connection between ancient wisdom and contemporary life.

5. Embracing the Infinite Protector

As we conclude our exploration of Shesha, it becomes clear that he represents more than just a mythological figure; he is a symbol of the eternal and infinite aspects of existence. His role as the Infinite Protector encapsulates the essence of cosmic continuity and renewal, offering valuable insights into the nature of the universe and our place within it.

- **Living the Principles:** Embracing Shesha's principles of stability, balance, and renewal invites us to live in harmony with the cosmic order. By aligning our actions and intentions with these principles, we contribute to the ongoing evolution of creation and support the perpetuation of cosmic harmony.

- **A Vision for the Future:** Shesha's final vision of the cosmos is one of eternal renewal and infinite protection. As we move forward, let us carry forward the lessons learned from Shesha's life, honoring his role as the guardian of cosmic stability and renewal.

In this way, Shesha's legacy endures, guiding us toward a future that embraces the infinite cycles of creation, supports the balance of the cosmic order, and upholds the timeless values that sustain the universe.

- The Journey of the Serpent King

Introduction

The Journey of the Serpent King, Shesha, is an epic narrative that traverses the realms of divine mythology, cosmic cycles, and spiritual evolution. As the primordial serpent in Hindu cosmology, Shesha's journey encapsulates the grand arc of creation, preservation, and dissolution, reflecting the profound truths about existence, time, and the universe. This chapter delves into the symbolic and metaphysical voyage of Shesha, exploring his role from the earliest moments of creation to his enduring presence in the cosmic order.

1. Origins of Shesha: The Primordial Serpent

The Cosmic Genesis:

Shesha's journey begins with his origins in the early stages of cosmic creation. As described in ancient texts, he emerges from the churning of the ocean, a primordial force embodying infinity and the cycles of time.

- **Creation Mythology:** Shesha's genesis is intertwined with the creation myths of Hinduism, where he is often depicted as emerging from the cosmic ocean, an embodiment of the primal forces that shape the universe. His form represents the infinite and the cyclical nature of existence, laying the foundation for his pivotal role in subsequent cosmic events.

- **Symbol of Infinity:** Shesha's serpentine form, coiled and extending endlessly, symbolizes the infinite nature of time and space. His presence is a constant reminder of the boundless aspects of the cosmos and the eternal cycles that govern creation.

2. Shesha as the Supporter of Vishnu

The Cosmic Bed:

One of Shesha's most prominent roles is as the divine bed upon which Vishnu rests. This association signifies his integral function in maintaining cosmic stability and supporting the divine activities of preservation and creation.

- **Role in Cosmic Stability:** Shesha's support of Vishnu illustrates his function as a stabilizer in the universe. His ability to provide a serene and supportive foundation for Vishnu underscores the importance of balance and harmony in the cosmic order.

- **Symbolic Significance:** The imagery of Shesha as Vishnu's bed conveys the deep connection between stability and divinity. His presence ensures that the divine functions of Vishnu are carried out in an environment of peace and equilibrium, reinforcing the notion of a well-ordered and harmonious cosmos.

3. Shesha in the Churning of the Ocean (Samudra Manthan)

The Ocean of Milk:

The Samudra Manthan, or churning of the ocean, is a pivotal episode in Hindu mythology where Shesha plays a crucial role. This event illustrates his participation in cosmic processes and his role in facilitating the emergence of divine nectar and treasures.

- **Cosmic Churning:** Shesha's involvement in the churning of the ocean highlights his role in the dynamic processes of creation and transformation. His support during this event symbolizes his contribution to the emergence of vital cosmic substances and beings.

- **Emergence of Amrita:** The churning of the ocean produces Amrita, the nectar of immortality, along with other divine treasures. Shesha's presence during this event emphasizes his role in facilitating the cosmic processes that sustain life and ensure continuity.

4. Shesha and the Cosmic Dissolution (Pralaya)

The End of an Era:

During the cosmic dissolution, or pralaya, Shesha's role becomes one of profound significance. As the universe undergoes dissolution, Shesha continues to provide support and stability, ensuring that the cosmic order is preserved for future creation.

- **Support During Dissolution:** In the periods of cosmic dissolution, Shesha remains a constant presence, ensuring that the universe's essence is preserved. His role during pralaya underscores his function as a protector and stabilizer even amidst the most transformative events.

- **Preparation for Renewal:** Shesha's presence during pralaya is a testament to his role in preparing the universe for the next cycle of creation. His continued support ensures that the foundation for future creation remains intact, facilitating the renewal of the cosmic order.

5. Shesha in the Avatars of Vishnu

The Divine Incarnations:

Shesha's role extends into the avatars of Vishnu, where he participates in the divine missions of preservation and transformation. Each avatar of Vishnu reflects different aspects of cosmic order, with Shesha's presence symbolizing the continuity of divine support.

- **Support in Various Avatars:** In each of Vishnu's avatars, Shesha's influence can be seen in various forms. His presence in these divine incarnations illustrates his integral role in supporting the preservation and restoration of cosmic balance through the ages.

- **Symbol of Continuity:** Shesha's involvement in the avatars of Vishnu highlights his role as a symbol of continuity and stability. His presence across different divine manifestations reinforces the notion of an enduring cosmic order and the eternal support provided by the primordial serpent.

6. Shesha in Iconography and Temples

The Sacred Depictions:

Shesha's representation in iconography and temples reflects his revered status in Hindu tradition. His depictions serve as a reminder of his divine role and the cosmic principles he embodies.

- **Symbolic Imagery:** The iconographic representations of Shesha, often depicted coiled around Vishnu or forming part of divine imagery, emphasize his role as a symbol of cosmic stability and infinite support. These depictions convey his eternal presence and the divine harmony he upholds.

- **Temples Dedicated to Shesha:** Temples dedicated to Shesha reflect his significance in Hindu worship and cultural traditions. These sacred spaces honor his role as a divine protector and supporter, providing a focal point for devotion and spiritual contemplation.

7. Shesha's Influence on Spiritual and Cultural Practices

Legacy and Inspiration:

Shesha's journey transcends mythology, influencing spiritual practices and cultural expressions. His symbolism continues to inspire devotion, artistic creation, and philosophical contemplation.

- **Spiritual Guidance:** Shesha's teachings offer valuable insights into spiritual growth and cosmic understanding. His role as the infinite protector provides guidance for navigating the spiritual path and embracing the principles of balance and renewal.

- **Cultural Impact:** The influence of Shesha extends into cultural practices, including rituals, art, and literature. His presence in these contexts reflects the enduring relevance of his symbolism and the continued reverence for the cosmic principles he represents.

8. The Future Vision of Shesha

Embracing Cosmic Principles:

As we look to the future, Shesha's journey offers a vision for the ongoing evolution of creation. His principles of stability, renewal, and interconnectedness provide a framework for understanding and navigating the future.

- **Guiding the Future:** Shesha's role as a symbol of eternal protection and cosmic balance can guide efforts to address contemporary challenges and foster a harmonious future. Embracing his principles can inspire collective efforts towards sustainability, spiritual growth, and global harmony.
- **Legacy of the Serpent King:** The legacy of Shesha continues to inspire and inform our understanding of the cosmos. His journey through creation, preservation, and dissolution reflects the timeless nature of cosmic principles and the enduring impact of the serpent king on the future of creation.

Conclusion

The journey of Shesha, the Infinite Protector, is a profound exploration of cosmic principles and divine support. From his origins in the primordial ocean to his role in the cycles of creation and dissolution, Shesha's presence is a testament to the eternal nature of the universe and the cosmic order. His influence on spiritual practices, cultural traditions, and the future of creation underscores the enduring significance of his symbolism.

As we reflect on Shesha's journey, we are reminded of the timeless principles of stability, renewal, and interconnectedness that guide the cosmos. The legacy of the serpent king continues to inspire and illuminate our understanding of the universe, offering a vision of harmony and continuity for generations to come.

- Shesha as a Symbol of Cosmic Truth

Introduction

In the vast and intricate tapestry of Hindu cosmology, Shesha emerges as a profound symbol of cosmic truth. His role as the primordial serpent transcends mere mythological narrative, embodying deeper spiritual and philosophical principles that reflect the fundamental nature of the universe. This chapter explores Shesha's symbolism as a representation of cosmic truth, examining how his form and attributes convey essential insights into the nature of reality, existence, and the divine order.

1. The Infinite Nature of Shesha

Symbolism of Infinity:

Shesha, often depicted as an infinitely coiled serpent, symbolizes the boundless and eternal aspects of the cosmos. His form, extending endlessly, reflects the infinite nature of time, space, and divine presence.

- **Endless Cycles:** Shesha's coiling form represents the cyclical nature of time and the eternal cycles of creation, preservation, and dissolution. His infinite coils suggest that the universe operates in an ongoing rhythm of birth, growth, decay, and renewal, illustrating the perpetual motion of cosmic processes.
- **Timelessness:** As an embodiment of infinity, Shesha signifies the timelessness that underlies the apparent flux of the material world. His unending presence serves as a reminder of the eternal truths that govern existence, beyond the transient phenomena of the physical realm.

2. The Cosmic Foundation and Stability

Support of the Divine:

Shesha's role as the divine couch or bed for Vishnu symbolizes his function as the foundation and stabilizer of the cosmos. His support for the divine ensures the stability and balance necessary for the universe to function harmoniously.

- **Foundation of Creation:** By supporting Vishnu, Shesha provides a stable base upon which the processes of creation and preservation occur. This role highlights the importance of a stable foundation in maintaining the cosmic order and the delicate balance required for the universe's functioning.

- **Symbol of Cosmic Order:** Shesha's presence as a stabilizer reflects the inherent order and harmony within the cosmos. His support ensures that the divine activities of Vishnu are carried out smoothly, emphasizing the interconnectedness of all cosmic elements and the underlying unity of the universe.

3. The Role in Cosmic Dissolution (Pralaya)

Endurance Through Transformation:

During cosmic dissolution, Shesha's enduring presence underscores his role as a symbol of continuity and preservation amid transformation. His support during pralaya, or the end of an era, demonstrates the persistence of cosmic principles even in times of upheaval.

- **Preservation of Essence:** Even as the universe undergoes dissolution, Shesha remains a constant presence, preserving the essential essence of existence. His role highlights the notion that, while the physical forms may change, the underlying principles and truths remain intact.

- **Preparation for Renewal:** Shesha's continued presence during dissolution signifies the readiness for the next cycle of creation. His role ensures that the cosmic order is preserved and prepared for renewal, reflecting the cyclical nature of existence and the eternal flow of cosmic energy.

4. Symbolism in the Churning of the Ocean (Samudra Manthan)

Facilitator of Divine Processes:

In the churning of the ocean, Shesha's participation reflects his role in facilitating the emergence of divine nectar and treasures. This event symbolizes the process of extracting essential truths and energies from the cosmic ocean.

- **Extraction of Amrita:** The churning of the ocean produces Amrita, the nectar of immortality, along with other divine substances. Shesha's involvement in this process emphasizes his role in bringing forth vital cosmic elements that sustain life and promote divine qualities.

- **Symbol of Transformation:** The Samudra Manthan represents the transformative processes that reveal hidden truths and energies. Shesha's presence in this event underscores his role in facilitating transformation and extraction of essential cosmic truths from the depths of existence.

5. The Serpent as a Cosmic Symbol

Representations in Sacred Texts:

Shesha's symbolism extends through various sacred texts, where he is depicted as a cosmic entity embodying essential truths about the nature of reality. His presence in scriptures reinforces his role as a symbol of the fundamental principles that govern the universe.

- **In the Vedas and Puranas:** Shesha is mentioned in the Vedas and Puranas as a primordial being whose form and attributes reflect cosmic truths. His role in these texts emphasizes his significance as a symbol of divine stability and eternal principles.
- **Philosophical Interpretations:** Philosophical interpretations of Shesha's symbolism reveal deeper insights into the nature of existence and the divine order. His depiction as a cosmic serpent serves as a metaphor for the infinite and eternal aspects of reality, offering a framework for understanding the nature of the universe.

6. Shesha's Influence on Spiritual Practices

Guidance for Spiritual Realization:

Shesha's symbolism extends into spiritual practices, where his role as a cosmic entity provides guidance for understanding and realizing higher truths. His presence in spiritual traditions reflects his influence on the pursuit of enlightenment and cosmic understanding.

- **Meditative Practices:** The image of Shesha can inspire meditative practices focused on the infinite and eternal aspects of existence. Contemplating Shesha's form and attributes can guide practitioners in their quest for spiritual realization and understanding of cosmic truths.
- **Symbolic Teachings:** The teachings associated with Shesha emphasize the importance of embracing the cyclical nature of existence and recognizing the underlying unity of all cosmic elements. His symbolism encourages individuals to align their spiritual practices with the principles of balance, renewal, and interconnectedness.

7. The Eternal Legacy of Shesha

Enduring Symbolism:

Shesha's legacy as a symbol of cosmic truth endures through various aspects of spiritual and cultural life. His presence continues to inspire and inform our understanding of the universe and our place within it.

- **Cultural Influence:** The symbolism of Shesha extends into cultural expressions, including art, literature, and rituals. His role as a cosmic entity continues to inspire creative and cultural endeavors that reflect the eternal principles he represents.
- **Spiritual Legacy:** The teachings and symbolism associated with Shesha offer timeless insights into the nature of reality and the divine order. His legacy serves as a reminder of the profound truths that underpin existence and the ongoing quest for spiritual understanding.

Conclusion

Shesha, the primordial serpent, embodies profound cosmic truths that transcend the boundaries of mythological narrative. As a symbol of infinity, stability, and cosmic continuity, Shesha represents the eternal principles that govern the universe. His role in various cosmic events, from creation to dissolution, highlights his significance as a symbol of cosmic truth and divine order.

The journey of Shesha reveals the timeless nature of existence and the interconnectedness of all cosmic elements. His presence in spiritual and cultural practices continues to inspire and guide our understanding of the universe, offering insights into the nature of reality and the eternal principles that sustain it. As we contemplate the infinite serpent, we are reminded of the profound truths that shape our existence and the enduring legacy of Shesha as the embodiment of cosmic truth.

Printed in Great Britain
by Amazon